OUTRUNNING YOUR EMOTIONS
Face Your Feelings, Find Your Power & Love Yourself

Written by the creator of
The Mighty Emotions Method™
Jiselle Gilliard Jegousse

DISCLAIMER: The author of this book does not dispense medical advice or prescribe the use of any technique as a form of treatment for physical, emotional, psychological or medical problems without the advice of a physician either directly or indirectly.

The information in this book is of a general nature and is only intended to help you in your quest for mental, emotional & spiritual well-being. The author and publisher assume no responsibility for your actions and specifically disclaim responsibility for any liability, physical, psychological or emotional damage personal or otherwise, which is incurred as a consequence directly or indirectly of the use and applications of any of the contents of this book.

COPYRIGHT © 2023 BY THE MIGHTY EMOTIONS CORPORATION. All rights reserved. No part of this publication may be reproduced, distributed or transmitted in any form or by any means, including photocopying, recording or other electronic or mechanical methods; nor may it be stored in a retrieval system, transmitted or otherwise be copied for public or private use without the prior written permission of the publisher, except in the case of brief quotations embodied in critical reviews and certain other non-commercial uses permitted by copyright law. For permission request, please send an email to mightyemotions@gmail.com.

Author: Jiselle Gilliard Jegousse
Publisher: The Mighty Emotions Corporation
Cover Design & Interior Design: Jiselle Gilliard Jegousse
Description: Outrunning Your Emotions/Jiselle Gilliard Jegousse 1st ed.
Website: Mightyemotions.com

ISBN e-book: 978-1-7780080-3-0
ISBN paperback: 978-1-7780080-2-3

Dedicated to you reader. You are not broken. You are far from it. May you finally heal and uncover your hidden light.

Contents

Introduction	9
PART ONE | Facing Your Feelings	19
1. Emotionally Underdeveloped	21
2. The Body Really Does Keep Score	30
3. Mighty Misconceptions	39
PART TWO | Finding Your Power	51
4. Our Personal Power	52
5. Sadness	63
6. Shame	69
7. Guilt	75
8. Fear	81
9. Anger	85
10. Disgust	91
11. Alignment	95
PART THREE | Loving Yourself	101
12. Relearning Self-Love	103
13. Our Core Needs	113
14. Letting Life Be Life	129
What Now?	137
Acknowledgments	139
About the Author	141
Appendix A: Ways of Honouring Your Emotions	143
Appendix B: Core Needs Wheel	144
Appendix C: Expanded Needs List	145
Appendix D: Sample Values List	146
Appendix E: Recognizing Our Emotions	147
Endnotes	150

Introduction

Twenty-eleven was the year I tried to kill myself. I was nineteen years old. My roommate found me unconscious in my bedroom and called 911. I woke up in the hospital, both disappointed and relieved that it hadn't worked. I didn't want to die, but I also didn't want to live. My seventy-two hour psych hold turned into a week in the psychiatric ward. I was monitored every day and to this day, I am very grateful for the care I received there. But I wasn't psychotic, I was miserable. The events of my life that led me to that moment haunted me every day.

I remember being happy as a very young child. For the first few years of my life I lived with my grandparents in the Caribbean. Those were the happiest times of my life. When I got older, my father sent for me to live with him and my stepmother in Canada. That is when the nightmare truly started (living with my father, not living in Canada). Initially, I was confused about meeting my stepmother and half-brothers who were total strangers to me. It did not take long before the abuse started, and it didn't end for years.

I think I hid it fairly well. I covered up my skin. I had zero friends at school, and we weren't allowed to play with other kids in the neighbourhood. I remember going to a babysitter at one point, but I never told anyone about what was happening. I didn't know what was normal or abnormal as a child. It was just my reality. I dreaded it, but I accepted it.

Eventually, the teachers at my school started to notice, and they called someone about it. The child services worker came for a visit. I remember them speaking to my father in the front doorway and then they left. Not long after that, my father packed up our bags and took us to live with my mother and stepfather. Finally, I was safe, I thought. No one would be hurting me anymore. Except that wasn't the reality.

Things started off good, but the good times didn't last very long. My mother and stepfather would drink, and become violent with each other. Their fighting was terrifying, but at least it wasn't directly at us. At least not at first. I remember my mother would frequently pass out on the couch surrounded by empty wine bottles. Being the oldest, I had to take care of my two younger siblings and make breakfast, lunches, and often dinners ourselves. I was an incredibly anxious child, always hyperalert. Loud noises would terrify me (It was only later that I understood that I had PTSD). I felt a huge responsibility to take care of my younger siblings and later to protect my mother from my stepfather's abuse.

During one of their more serious fights, he knocked her unconscious, and left. I watched my mother unresponsive on the floor, and called 911 while my two younger sisters cowered together crying. The paramedics came and took my mother to the hospital. I stayed behind with my sisters while the police contacted an adult to look after us so they could focus on tracking down my stepfather.

All of this happened before I was thirteen years old. No one ever talked to me about it or tried to help me understand what had happened. I was left on my own to make sense of all of it. I watched the adults in my life deal with their unhappiness by drinking. At twelve years old, I began sneaking vodka from my stepfather's liquor cabinet. For whatever reason, he never seemed to notice. If he did, he probably thought it was my mom.

With more practice under my belt, I got better at hiding what was going on at home. I became outgoing and fun primarily thanks to the alcohol numbing my anxiety. No one outside seemed to know what was happening. A friend of mine introduced me to marijuana at thirteen years old. Thank God. I'm not sure what would have happened if I didn't have these tools for escape. Somehow I was still expected to function, go to school, take care of my sisters, and be an adult before I had even finished puberty. It was all too much. Once I found ways to numb, it became manageable. I understood why people turned to drugs and alcohol. I could stop feeling my emotions so intensely, and carry on with my day. Drugs made me feel in control.

I quickly became dependent on alcohol and marijuana. I would go off with random older students in high school and get high at lunch, then go to math class. I started to lose some of my good friends, but I didn't care. I didn't need connection with other people anymore. I had found drugs and alcohol.

School was actually my saving grace. I had always loved reading. My first addiction was fantasy fiction because it allowed me to escape into other worlds. (Thank you JK Rowling & CS Lewis!) I loved reading historical fiction, and learning in all my classes. When I went to school, I stayed as long as possible so I didn't have to go home. I'd go to the library or find after school groups to give me an excuse to hang around. I became a musical theatre nerd, and was part of every school performance.

Outrunning Your Emotions

However, as I progressed in my drug and alcohol addiction, I started going to school less. I realized I could still get good grades even if I didn't attend every day, and I calculated exactly what my attendance needed to be to graduate. I graduated a year early.

This new independence led to a lot of clashing with my mother and stepfather. They had gone from being mostly absent figures in my life to trying to set household rules. My mother had discovered religion and stopped drinking heavily. We had to go to church every week. My stepfather never came. Suddenly, I had a curfew, and had to inform them of where I was going.

Naturally, I rebelled. I was full of unprocessed anger, shame and grief with no one to help me find resolution. We started fighting. First verbally; then physically. I took my anger out on everyone, including my younger sisters. (I have made amends to my sisters, but I will forever be deeply dismayed having treated them that way. They didn't deserve it.)

After one particularly violent fight between my stepfather and I, my mother kicked me out. She told me that she was not giving up her life, i.e. nice house, husband, etc. It wasn't the first time she had kicked me out, and I had gone to stay at a friend's house for the night. This time, it was permanent. She put my dirty laundry into a garbage bag, and locked the door. I called a guy I was seeing at the time who picked me up so we could go get high. I didn't tell him what had happened. When he dropped me off at the house the next day, I waited till he left, grabbed my garbage bag of clothes that I'd left at the side of the house and went to a friend's house to do my laundry.

I had nowhere to live. Thankfully, I had been working since I was fifteen because I could never ask my parents for money. (I know fifteen isn't the legal working age, but I got a cash job working at a pizza parlour and local paper route). When I turned sixteen, I got legal jobs working in clothing stores at the mall. By the time my mother kicked me out, I was working in a large grocery store. My friend let me do my laundry at her house, and I rode the bus all night until it was time to start my shift. Fortunately, the grocery store had a staff room with lockers, and a shower.

Riding the bus, using the bathroom at my job, and Tim Hortons became my life. I had no safe place to stay. My addiction had also graduated from weed and alcohol to opiates. I could not function without them. I stayed with various men that would help me out in exchange for drugs, and, of course, physical companionship. I didn't care. I was numb to all of it.

Outrunning Your Emotions

Eventually, the pastor of the church that my mother attended allowed me to move in with her and her family. She adopted me, and gave me a home. I wish I could say I stopped doing drugs, and cleaned up my act, but that wouldn't be the truth. I remember feeling such intense guilt from being strung out in their home, but my drugs were my lifeline.

Eventually it was time to go to university out of town. School had always been my saving grace. I was excited to go to university in a completely new city where I could get my life together. University was going to be the place where I turned my life around. Except it wasn't.

Everything fell on my shoulders financially. I was working at the school, and attending full-time studies. I lived off of my small salary, scholarship, and student loans. I loved being at school. I loved learning. But the pressure of it all terrified me. Here I was, a black girl from a broken home at an ivy league school on a scholarship. I didn't feel worthy of it, and wanting to avoid my shame only led me to use more drugs.

My drug use got worse as my first year of school came to an end. It didn't help that my university had a notorious party culture, and I would frequently wake up in the student drunk tank, and stumble back to my dorm having no memory of the day before.

Blacking out was a frequent occurrence. I tried getting help from the therapists at the school. After one session, I decided I was going to just continue self-medicating. As the end of the year approached, I realized I would need to find somewhere to live the next year. I made the decision not to continue with my studies and moved back to my hometown.

I got a few jobs, but my full-time job was my addiction. The year after I left University was one of the most traumatic of my life. Most of it, I can't remember. I woke up in the hospital, and police station several times from being picked up on the street. The only reason I wasn't charged with public drunkenness was because the officer that picked me up was a friend of my mother. (The Universe works in funny ways.)

Men became my financial supply when I couldn't keep my day jobs anymore. This led to toxic, and abusive relationships, and a lot of sexual trauma. I wasn't hiding the mess I was in anymore. It was obvious. I look back now at Facebook posts of my party days where I am smiling, but it was the most miserable time of my life. I had an over-active social life because I could only be alone with myself until the high wore off. My phone was constantly ringing, I loved being the life of the party, but the truth was I hated my life.

Outrunning Your Emotions

This is what led to my failed suicide attempt. There are so many details that I have left out, some because I generally have no memory of them, others because the details aren't what's important. If you're still reading this, I'm sure that you'll agree that what I've already described is enough hardship for any one person to take.

The truth is, I started slowly killing myself the day I started sneaking vodka from the liquor cabinet at twelve years-old. Addiction is called a slow suicide for a reason. No one becomes a drug addict because they feel great on the inside. It was absolutely my choice to use drugs and alcohol to cope. To my mind, my options were being a drug addict and feeling "good" some of the time or living in mental anguish and emotional misery all of the time. I choice the better of the two.

Thankfully, when I was released from the hospital, I was given a third choice. After the psychologist cleared me to leave I remember standing outside the hospital smoking a cigarette, and thinking that I didn't have a life that I wanted to go back to. My grandparents had somehow gotten the number to reach me at the hospital, and they offered to buy me a one-way ticket back to the country of my birth. I thought about how living with them as a child was the happiest time of my life. Here I was being offered help and I took it. I left everything behind and within a week I was on a plane back home.

I'll never forget the look on my grandmother's face when she saw me walk off the plane. She tried her best to not show it, but I could see in her eyes that she was horrified. I was a shell of a human. Dark spots all over my skin, thin as a rail with my black wool coat swallowing me (it had been February in Canada when I left). More than anything I was relieved. To finally be with people that cared for me. No longer having to always be on guard.

The first few months back home I mostly slept. I stayed in bed all day and night while my grandmother came to sit and talk to me. I was severely depressed, and she let me be. She didn't try to cure me. She just loved me unconditionally. Every day she brought me food, encouraged me to take a bath, and mostly left me alone. My younger cousin would also come and talk to me. I wasn't very kind to her in those early days. I was detoxing from drugs, angry at the world, relieved to be somewhere safe, but I held on to so much shame. I thought about how I had thrown my life away. Or so I thought.

Eventually, the nurturing I received brought me back to life. My

Outrunning Your Emotions

Grandmother let me share what had happened to me honestly without judgment. I know it must have been hard for her to hear what I was sharing, but she never shared her opinion. She just loved me. For the first time in a long time, I had safety, freedom, meaning and connection. I started feeling positive emotions and was able to stay sober. I had food every day, people that loved me, and I didn't need to carry the world on my shoulders anymore.

I stopped doing drugs, regained my health, got a job, and even went back to school. I made healthy friends, and started enjoying life again. No one cared about my past, they were just supportive of my healing in the present.

I came back to Canada. I felt ready to be independent again. My grandparents weren't thrilled about it, but without their blessing, I left. Their worries were justified because not long after I came back to Canada did I reconnect with a toxic ex-boyfriend. I bet you can guess what happened.

Yep-I started drinking and using drugs again. The relationship fell apart and so did I. By this point I had gone to some therapy, but I hadn't gained the tools to prepare me for being on my own again. I still didn't know any other way of dealing with difficult emotions.

My lifestyle started to take a turn for the worse. This time, I didn't let it get too far before I confided in a friend that I was struggling. We were close, and she observed my decline. She happened to have a partner who was a member of Narcotics Anonymous, and took me to my first meeting.

Accepting help from my grandparents had at least shown me that telling safe people when I was in trouble, and being open to their help was a smart decision. I took the help, and started my journey of recovery.

It was on this journey that I began to realize how emotionally fragile I was. Without drugs and alcohol to manage my moods, I was erratic. Every day brought extreme anxiety. Thanks to the recovery program I was in, I could always find a meeting. These meetings gave me a couple hours a day where I could quiet the noise in my head, and talk about what I was experiencing with people who just held space for me.

I got my first mentor in the program. A lovely woman who contributed so much to my early healing. We went to meetings, and women's retreats together. I would pour my heart out to her and she would always receive me with grace and acceptance. It was an amazing way to heal from the past. It gave me a safe community that loved me and encouraged me. I was able to release a lot of my pain.

However, I would experience everything as a crisis for me. My emotions would be so intense and I was convinced that I had to be broken. I became obsessed with fixing myself through self-help and spiritual healing. I found new therapists, picked up yoga, started meditating and filled journal after journal, both with my recovery work and the work I was doing in therapy. I started attending several different recovery groups because I believed my emotional distress was due to me just having too many mental problems.

All the work I was doing helped me get through the day sober, but it did not cure me of 'negative' emotions and thoughts like I wanted it to. I had incredibly low self-esteem. I just thought I was inherently flawed. Why else would my parents treat me so poorly? Maybe I was born broken beyond repair?

Eventually, I was tired of always cycling between feeling amazing, and being depressed. It was exhausting. I couldn't understand why my tools weren't working. I was taking action, looking at my thoughts, but something was missing. One day, I decided I was too tired to run anymore. It just didn't make sense that nothing I did freed me from my "negative" emotions. I became determined to find an answer. I refused to accept that I would always be in this cycle. There had to be another way.

So I started with the one thing that no one had ever helped me understand, my emotions. I began to study trauma and its effects on the body. I learned about the various nervous system states. Most importantly, I sat with my emotions so I could become familiar and safe with them.

Rather than turning to one of my coping techniques, the next time I had big feelings show up, I sat. I observed. I noticed what sadness felt like in my body. I cried. I swayed. I yawned. I hummed. I let my body process it all. I didn't think about it. I surrendered to it. It felt like floating in the ocean, and I didn't drown.

On the other side of that surrender, I found myself in a neutral, and grounded state. My mind was clear. Suddenly, I started having realisations that had never occurred to me before. Questions that I had never asked myself before like, "what do you need?", and "how can you take care of yourself right now?" The more I practised processing my emotions in this way, the better I began taking care of myself.

In the years that followed, I practised more and more. I threw a lot of adult tantrums when I didn't want to face my emotions. I caused harm to people I loved, but I kept practising. I became less reactive. People would tell me how "spiritual" I seemed. I would share the insights I was having, and people would tell me that it helped them. I didn't call it a method just yet, I just continued to refine it. When something difficult would happen, and big feelings would come, I would practise. Eventually, I developed a positive relationship with my emotions. I could embrace sadness, anger and guilt. I began to understand that my emotions were serving me, and I trusted them.

When the world went into a pandemic, and I got pregnant, it was time to really apply my method. It was deep and intense work. My relationship with fear and shame got so much better. My method got more refined. I understood myself and my emotions more deeply. I continued sharing what I was learning, and it continued to help others. I decided to get a specialization in positive psychology which confirmed what I had learned from my emotions - that they were there to help me, not harm me. I learned about the difference between emotions, feelings, and moods. I learned about the power of positive emotions.

Then I began getting certified. My certifications in Psychological First-Aid and Emotional CPR taught me how to hold space for people experiencing trauma. My own experience showed me that no one who is struggling is broken, they just feel like they are. I started working with clients via referrals. People would come to me struggling, and I would help them see themselves as human beings deserving of compassion and grace. I would teach them to understand and work with their emotions and to take better care of themselves. It helped them the same way it helped me.

This is what I will be sharing with you in this book. I started by sharing my story so you can understand that this has been a journey for me. Not just a journey to better understanding my emotions, but a journey to understanding that there is nothing wrong with me. I am valuable, worthy, and deserving of care - just like you.

I want my work to show you that there is nothing wrong with you. You are not broken. Life may have taken you off course, but you have the power inside you to set a better course. You are a beautiful soul who is here to share your light with the world. If it's possible for me to overcome my past traumas, become more resilient, and love myself it is possible for you.

In Part One, I am going to help you understand what your emotions truly are. We will explore where they come from, how we

Outrunning Your Emotions

experience them, and what misconceptions have to be unlearned so we can fully embrace them.

In Part Two, I am going to teach you the Mighty Emotions Method™, so you can begin to practise it in your own life. I am going to share what each emotion has to teach us, and what actions you can take to respond to your emotions in healthy ways. I encourage you to develop your own relationship with your emotions, and listen to what they have to say.

Finally, in Part Three, we are going to talk about self-love, self-compassion, and self-care. We will dive deeper into what our core needs are, the main obstacles that prevent our needs from getting met, and build out a plan to have more harmony in our lives.

While I will be referring to sources where appropriate, most of what I share is going to be from first-hand experience. Feel free to use what resonates and leave the rest. I speak in the affirmative because I am passionate and confident about what I teach. It has helped the many clients I have worked with and people who had heard me speak. However, never forget that *you* are the authority of your life. I encourage you to form your own opinions. In fact, form *new* opinions as you read this book.

Our mission at Mighty Emotions is to help anyone suffering overcome their past traumas, become emotionally empowered and nurture themselves. Reading this book will get you started on that journey. The resources at the back of the book will provide further direction. You are here and the future is bright.

Three principles that can help you on this journey as they helped me on mine are: honesty, open mindedness and willingness. The courage to be radically honest with yourself. The ability to be open-minded. The willingness to take different actions. My hope is this book will be a resource for you. That you will pick it up when you are struggling with emotional overwhelm, and it will help you return to wholeness within yourself. Thank you for letting me be a part of your journey. Be gentle with yourself.

Jiselle Gilliard, Emotions Coach
Creator of The Mighty Emotions Method
mightyemotions.com

| PART ONE |

Facing Your Feelings

1

Emotionally Underdeveloped

Emotional immaturity is a hallmark of our current society. People would rather talk about politics and race relations than be vulnerable about what they feel. The demand for emotional support far outweighs the supply. The World Health Organization states that in the past decade (until 2017) mental health conditions and substance use disorders have seen a 13% increase[1]. It doesn't come as a surprise that many people were completely unprepared for what happened in 2020.

More and more, adults and children are being diagnosed with anxiety disorders. A scientific study found that despite there being many intervention strategies today, anxiety and depressive disorders remain a leading cause of burden globally.[2] People everywhere are struggling emotionally and not getting the support they need. For all the talk of mental health in our pop culture, we rarely address emotions, even though the definition of mental health is "a person's condition with regard to their psychological and *emotional* well-being".

How did we get so lost?

We are all born with emotions. Our first cry is a critical moment in the delivery room. For medical professionals, it's a sign that you're able to breathe on your own. For you, the infant, it's a sign of the displeasure of no longer being in the safe, nourishing womb of your mother. It is an expression of grief, fear, and disgust.

We may be different in many ways, but all of us have the same core emotions. They are with us from the moment we are born until the moment we die. Our emotions are our most primal instincts.

Even sociopaths have emotions.[3] I truly believe our world would be a better place if we understood this.

Even the 'Experts' Are Confused

A simple Google search for "what is an emotion" is going to give you many conflicting responses. Author Brené Brown opens up in her book *Atlas of the Heart* by acknowledging how vast the research is about emotions.[4] In it she states that this is due to emotions being studied from various angles, i.e. medically, psychologically, philosophically, etc.

Experts can't even agree on the number of emotions we have. The research ranges anywhere from seven to twenty-seven and beyond. The general consensus is that there are seven core emotions corresponding to seven universal facial expressions. [5]Even still, experts can't agree on what the seven core emotions are. Some say guilt is a core emotion, while others say contempt is one. Regardless of what experts consider an emotion or not, they all agree that developing emotional intelligence is important.

Where Development Begins

As human beings, we need certain conditions in order to develop and mature well. In the right environments with all our needs satisfied, we don't just survive- we thrive. To prosper is our birthright. All of us deserve lives where we have what we need to flourish.

If not, we can't develop the necessary life skills to self-regulate and process our emotions fully. These basic life skills are needed to help us navigate challenging moments. Without them, our mental and physical well-being suffers.

Learning about early childhood development taught me a lot about how emotional development works. Healthy development in children is defined as being able to grow up having their social, emotional, and educational needs met.[6] When children have their needs deprived, they are shown to have long-term impacts that include depression, reduced self-control, and poor resilience. [7]

Do you know any adults who suffer from depression, reduced self-control, and poor resilience? I know at least one who did for years: *me*.

When I began my recovery journey, I was extremely emotionally fragile. I threw more tantrums than a toddler. I was triggered and offended by seemingly everything. I was isolated. I went through cycles of depression. Everyday life was extremely challenging for me mentally. I was barely functioning.

My emotions were completely out of control, and I had no clue what to do about it. I couldn't understand why I struggled so much while it seemed so easy for other people. They seemed to hold it together. I thought 'holding it together' and being stoic (i.e., seemingly unaffected emotionally) was a sign of maturity.

I didn't know that my emotions were normal in response to what I was experiencing. I thought I only felt the way I felt because of my traumatic childhood. I thought that my brain was broken. It left me feeling powerless.

Ignorance Leads to Immaturity

"Emotional immaturity is a person's inability to express or cope with emotions that are serious in nature. People who are emotionally immature may also overreact to situations or have trouble controlling their emotions."[8] This was certainly true in my case. When I experienced intense emotions, they would completely consume me and seemed to last for weeks at a time.

Research suggests that we become emotionally immature when we have a difficult childhood and parts of our brain are left underdeveloped.[9] It is proven that a difficult childhood leaves us with a smaller hippocampus (the part of our brain mainly associated with memory).

This doesn't mean that we can't later develop it with the right education and support. Emotional maturation is not restricted by our physiology. The development of skills such as self-regulation and critical thinking can still happen later in life. After all, the brain is a muscle. We develop it by stimulating it with the right information and thinking critically, taking action, and repeatedly iterating.

Acquiring and developing any skill requires the right knowledge and instruction of how to effectively apply said knowledge. The first step is learning what your emotions are. Then, you learn how to respond and practice doing so until it's second nature. This builds your mental dexterity over time. The more we develop our ability to process our emotions, the more our brains develop.

Most intervention strategies are short-sighted and focused on teaching people to develop coping skills (i.e., how to get from one moment to the next). We need to be helping people develop *understanding*, get to the root cause so they can find resolution. This is exactly why I created the Mighty Emotions Method™.

When I first began using this method in my daily life, it would take me days to fully process an emotion. Now, thanks to the years of daily application I have, I can recover from intense feelings in under an hour at times. In fact, I rarely ever have intense emotions or depressive episodes because I've gotten so good at listening to my emotions even when they are just a whisper. If we learn to address them early on, it saves us a lot of suffering.

I observe my clients develop their emotion management skills as well. When we first start working together, it takes them some time to really feel comfortable with the practice. However, week after week of taking small but mighty actions, when faced with challenges in their lives, leads to powerful shifts. Months later, they find themselves more resilient than they initially would have believed possible!

Do we outgrow our emotions?

Most emotion coaches work with children. (Yes, an emotions coach is a real title. I didn't make it up!) I choose to work with adults because they need the most help. Age alone does not affect our emotional development, but expectations change as we age. For some reason, after a certain age, we're expected to no longer require emotional support from others. We're supposed to be completely self-sufficient (unless there is an obvious reason that would grant you accommodation) even if we weren't taught how. This leaves us with no choice but to pretend that everything is fine, lest we be ostracized.

There seems to be all these criteria for what makes it okay for someone to struggle emotionally. You did not need to experience extreme conditions like I did to end up emotionally underdeveloped. Many people who had seemingly "normal" childhood's do not develop healthy emotion management skills. Why? Because they weren't given the support they needed. Often they were left on their own to make sense of what they felt. Or their emotions were dismissed or belittled.

I know many people who were not physically abused, but they were neglected. They spent a lot of time on their own. They were bullied. They were shamed and judged when they had an emotional outburst.

Some people grew up in extremely strict conditions as children.

Outrunning Your Emotions

They were only accepted if they suppressed how they really felt and behaved a certain way. Anything outside of that was shunned, or they were punished.

Not everyone grew up in homes where they could ask for what they needed. Not everyone grew up in homes where they saw and experienced healthy emotional responses. Not every child has emotionally mature parents.

We do not stop having emotional reactions to life, and our emotions are never going to go away. We deserve to continually be supported as well as get trained on how to process our emotions.

Getting to Know Our Emotions

When I realized that nothing I did got rid of my emotions, I started asking different questions. Up until that point, I had been asking questions like "Why did they treat me that way?" "What do I need to do to feel better?" And most commonly: "What is wrong with me?"

These questions did not serve my emotional development. I remained depressed and emotionally fragile. Revisiting the past over and over kept me thinking in circles and feeling worse about myself.

I saw professionals and was given tools to reframe things. I was given methods to help me cope. All I wanted was to make my uncomfortable emotions disappear permanently. I wanted to outgrow my emotions.

This led me to study the work of American psychologist Paul Ehkman, who identified that there are seven core emotions, which evolved to help us survive daily life.[10] (We also have complex or compound emotions that are combined elements of our primary emotions.)

These are the emotions that have helped me the most as I have healed from the past and learned to navigate life. These are the emotions that I help my clients learn to trust. They are: sadness, anger, guilt, shame, fear, disgust, and alignment.

You may be thinking, but what about resentment? Disappointment? Or anxiety? Studying positive psychology (the study of what makes life worth living), helped me understand that in addition to emotions, we also have *feelings* and *moods*.

Feelings and emotions are *not* the same things. The nuances between emotions, feelings, and moods are important to understand.[11] Emotions are our primal instincts. They are the signals our body sends us

Outrunning Your Emotions

to let us know when our needs aren't being met (i.e., sadness). Feelings are the ways we describe our experiences. They are our impressions of what we are experiencing. They are created from our thoughts (i.e., disappointment). Moods are temporary states created by external sources (i.e., being in a low, demotivated mood because it's raining outside).

A great tool which illustrates how emotions and feelings are different is the Emotions and Feelings wheel. In the middle of the wheel are the core emotions, and as you move further from the centre there are different *feelings* related to each core emotion. For example, anger would be in the centre, while annoyance or frustration would be in the wider circle.

This is a tool originally created by American psychologist Dr. Robert Plutchik. Today, you can find many online by doing a simple Google search. I also have a free video breaking down how to use this tool to identify what you're feeling in my free resources section at members.mightyemotions.com.

The definition of an emotion is "an instinctive or intuitive feeling as distinguished from reasoning or knowledge". Our emotions are biological instincts, but my experience teaches me that they are more than that. Our emotions are not just tools for survival. They are tools to help us thrive.

All those years of surviving were the most miserable years of my life. Numbing my emotions for a decade with drugs and alcohol didn't prevent me from 'surviving' either. I was completely disconnected from my intuition, but I was surviving. Our survival doesn't depend on whether all our needs are met, but our happiness does. Our well-being does.

Let's use an example of two plants. One of the plants is in a pot that is too small for its roots to grow. It's not getting adequate sunlight. No one remembers to water it consistently, and it's often neglected.

Now think about a plant on a lush plant wall. This plant is getting adequate light and water. It is connected to other plants and is admired every day.

The first plant described is surviving. The plant on the wall is flourishing. Of these two plants, which do you think is going to grow well? I know the answer seems obvious when we use the example of plants, but it's a good illustration of what growth requires. Just like plants, we have certain core needs if we want to grow. Plants have needs for sunlight, water, certain nutrients, etc.

Outrunning Your Emotions

We have physical, emotional, mental, and spiritual needs that help us get through life, and whether or not these needs are met will determine what emotions we feel most strongly. A buildup of unprocessed emotions means a buildup of unmet needs. This is why it's so important that we learn to feel.

How do we begin to heal?

Have you ever heard the expression "you need to feel in order to heal?" This is one hundred percent the case, but most of us settle for relief instead of true healing. We often don't even realize we have another option.

Personally, I spent years wanting to control my emotions. I did not know I could trust them because I had never let myself truly experience them. We don't trust things that are unfamiliar. To our minds, uncertainty equals danger. It doesn't help that we are taught to mistrust what we feel. In fact, it's highly encouraged!

We learn that some emotions are "good" and "acceptable" while others are "bad" and "shameful". This leads us to chase certain emotions and reject others. We falsely believe we can experience some without experiencing others. The problem is that rejecting or avoiding our emotions doesn't eliminate them.

What we believe about our emotions determines how we respond to them. In order to heal, we have to be willing to unlearn. The more I opened myself up to seeing my emotions in a new way, the easier it became to feel them, no matter how challenging.

Some of our emotions are comforting, and some are uncomfortable. Positive psychology highlights the benefits of both the pleasant and unpleasant emotional experiences. "When we are able to accept, embrace, and exploit both our positive and our negative emotions, we give ourselves the best chance to live a balanced, meaningful life."[12]

I didn't feel like my life was meaningful when I was spending all of my time pushing my emotions away instead of approaching them with curiosity.

Healing is not just about getting temporary relief. It is about being restored to a state of wholeness. A state of optimal well-being. When we haven't processed our emotions, we live in a fragmented way. Trauma, here defined as a buildup of unprocessed emotions over time, disconnects our minds from our bodies.

My clients often come to me after having spent so much time living in their minds and not knowing how to feel their emotions. True healing helps us integrate our whole selves. Accepting and embracing all of my emotions has been the key to my healing and my resilience. Allowing myself to have the full range of emotional experiences has led to me living a more fulfilling life.

Every time I surrendered to the uncomfortable emotions, I opened myself up to experience pleasurable feelings and emotions as well. On the other side of sadness, shame, guilt, anger, fear, and disgust was alignment. (I use alignment as a catch all for the positive feelings of love, gratitude, and joy).

Life started to have more meaning. I felt more connected to myself. My relationships got better. I was able to set boundaries easily. I trusted myself, and my self-esteem improved. I no longer had severe social anxiety or depressive episodes on a regular basis. I felt free. Free to be authentically myself. Free to make decisions that were good for me. Free to try new things and safe to do so.

I have watched as my clients' learning to feel has allowed them to heal from their past as well. One of my male clients came to me because he struggled with suppressing his emotions since the death of his mother. He had never fully grieved it. Every time I saw him, he would be wearing black and be really closed off. After a month of working through the Mighty Emotions Method™ with me, he started showing up on our calls wearing colour and being playful. It was like talking to a new person.

He told me he hadn't been playful in his life since he was a kid. We began processing the grief and shame he held about the death of his mother, and he began trusting those emotions. Weeks later, he told me how for the first time ever, he had a vulnerable conversation with his father where they shared how they felt about it. It brought them closer together.

He began to feel better about himself and started getting noticed at work. This led to him getting promoted to manager. He used the Mighty Emotions Method to work through the fear and self-doubt that came with this promotion. One day, he sent me a long message telling me that he had freedom from anxiety that had plagued him his entire life.

He had come out of a situation in which he previously would have felt low self-worth, and only after did he realize how confidently he had handled himself. He cried tears of gratitude for that moment.

Outrunning Your Emotions

All because he had been willing to take the small but mighty action to rebuild his relationship with his emotions.

Building a healthy relationship with our emotions is like building any healthy relationship. When you first meet someone, you don't yet feel safe with them. The more you have good experiences with them, the more at ease you feel with them. Most of us panic when we experience our emotions because we are emotionally underdeveloped. Fortunately, we are not doomed. We can and should learn to embrace and work with our emotions.

Emotion management is not about controlling our emotions. It's about being intentional with how we *respond* to them. It is a necessary life skill. You experience emotions every day. They are unavoidable parts of being alive. When you know how to manage your emotions, they become an inner compass that is always guiding you from misalignment to a state of optimal well-being. Not paying attention to them or doing our best to avoid them causes internal and external chaos. Now that we understand what they are, let's look at how we experience them.

2

The Body *Really Does* Keep Score

Our emotions are energy, and they exist as part of a system within our body. There is a reason we link emotions to water in various metaphors. We feel a difference whether they are flowing or accumulating within our bodies.

In their book *Discovering Psychology*, authors Don Hockenbury and Sandra E. Hockenbury suggest that an emotion is a complex psychological state that involves three distinct components: a subjective experience, a physiological response, and a behavioural or expressive response.[13]

These three main phases of processing our emotions take us on a journey from awareness, to integration, and finally, resolution. The awareness phase is when we notice our physical discomfort. The integration phase is when we cognitively process what we are experiencing, trying to make sense of things. The resolution phase is when we take action to address the root cause of the emotion (i.e., our unmet need) and close the emotional loop.

When an emotion is triggered and we don't know how to process it, we either attempt to deny it or distract ourselves from it. This keeps us repeatedly cycling through each phase because we take actions that don't lead to resolution. We may achieve temporary relief, but end up back at the awareness phase shortly thereafter because we never completed the process.

Do emotions come from the brain?

You may be hearing a lot of talk about the nervous system right now. Let's talk about what the nervous system is and the role it plays in helping us process our emotions. Our nervous system connects our minds to our bodies. It allows our minds and bodies to communicate with each other and help us get what we need using sensory information.

The mind and body were designed to communicate with each other, each with their own role to play in our survival. Our central nervous system comprises the mind (including the brain) and our peripheral nervous system comprises the somatic and autonomic nervous systems (housed in the body). The two states of our autonomic nervous system are sympathetic (i.e., fight or flight) and parasympathetic (i.e., rest and digest or open & receptive).

When these systems are effectively communicating with each other, the process is something like this:
1. The unconscious mind absorbs sensory information and detects whether our needs are being met. It sends a signal through the body that we have an unmet need.
2. The subconscious mind interprets the meaning of the body's signals based on information our unconscious mind has absorbed from the past, and causes us to have a reaction.
3. The conscious mind analyzes the body's signal, weighs our options and makes an intentional decision about what action to take. When that action addresses our unmet need, the process is complete. If the action does not address our unmet need, we continue to feel dysregulated and turn to coping mechanisms to gain relief.

This process either happens intentionally or unintentionally. We have a subconscious reaction and then consciously decide to respond. This system works the same way when we have a need to eat, sleep, or use the bathroom. When we are hungry, our body sends a signal. Our mind notices this signal and is able to translate it into instructions to get food. Our body then carries out the actions of finding, preparing, and eating food. When we feel satiated, the process is complete.

If our body sends the signal to our mind that we are hungry, but the mind does not correctly interrupt this signal, our sensation of hunger becomes more and more intense because our body knows the longer we go without eating, the more it threatens our well-being. When the signal becomes more aggressive, we go into some version of fight or flight (or another trauma response/protective behaviour.)

Outrunning Your Emotions

Our Mind Is a Powerful Computer

The mind is not the same as the brain. When we refer to the mind, we are discussing the psyche. The psyche is our psychological structure. It goes beyond the brain. It encompasses the human soul and spirit.

We've already discussed that the mind has two main jobs when it comes to processing our emotions. First, it translates the signals of the body communicating a need, and then it produces instructions for us to perform actions that meet the body's requests.

Most of us have heard of the conscious, subconscious and unconscious layers of mind. This is a theory founded by controversial psychologist Sigmund Freud, founder of psychoanalytic theory. His theory is that there are layers of the mind, each with its own roles and functions.[14]

The conscious mind allows us to *respond*. It enables us to analyze, gather information, solve problems, and make decisions about the best action to take. The subconscious mind causes us to *react* to situations based on our core beliefs about how the world works. You may also hear this referred to as our "mental models" of the world.

We need the subconscious mind in order to react quickly to circumstances because the conscious mind needs more time to process before we can take action. Our bodies (unconscious mind) communicate in sensations while our brain (conscious mind) communicates in symbols. The subconscious mind is there to interpret and translate the sensations into symbols that the conscious mind can use to take action.

All our experiences begin at the unconscious layer of mind. Anything we see, hear, taste, touch, or smell is automatically absorbed and stored in our unconscious mind as sensory information and later used by our subconscious mind to make sense of things. Our conscious mind can then be used to challenge what our subconscious mind has determined. This allows us to gather more information in order to take deliberate action.

Let's use hunger again as an example. We are absorbing sensory information about food all of the time. We see images of different foods. We smell different scents. We hear the sounds of different food being prepared. We taste different textures and flavours. All of this sensory information is bypassing our conscious mind and being absorbed by our unconscious mind and stored for later use.

When we lack sustenance (i.e., food), our unconscious mind (i.e., our bodies) sends the signal. Our subconscious mind interprets this signal based on how we felt similarly in the past. We will then react in an automatic, familiar way. Our subconscious mind will know if there are specific nutrients that our bodies are missing, and we will experience that consciously as a craving for a certain type of food. Our conscious mind steps in when we pause, reflect, and choose *what* we would like to eat or how we would like to get food. For example, should we go to the store, find the right ingredients, prepare the meal, and eat the meal (or, let's be honest, scroll on Uber or Postmates until we find something, order it, have it delivered, and then enjoy it). Our conscious mind helps us make better decisions.

Once we have deliberately chosen a response, this is stored in our subconscious to help us automatically react similarly the next time. This is how our psyche and nervous system work together to help us survive. The process works the same way with our emotions.

Unpacking Our Subconscious Mind

Two 'features' of our subconscious mind are important to understand. These are two filters that our subconscious mind uses when making sense of our body's signals. The first filter is our limiting beliefs. The second filter is semiotics. Both these filters contribute to how our emotions are processed and how we view our world.

A limiting belief is a narrow perception we have that lacks nuance. Black-or-white thinking. Either-Or thinking. These are examples of limiting ways of thinking.

When we do not seek additional information about a subject, we are limited in our understanding. This becomes a limiting belief. Our subconscious minds are there to interpret (i.e., make sense of) the sensory information (i.e., things we hear, see, and experience). If we don't get all the relevant information, we make assumptions based on the information that we do have.

As children, for example, our worldview is very limited because our experiences are limited. We don't realise, that our parents are human beings just like us. We see them as these powerful figures because they have authority and we depend on them to get our needs met. As we mature and see ourselves as more autonomous, we begin to see our parents as our peers and depend on them less for getting our needs met. However, if we never learn to see ourselves as powerful, we will continue to have our childlike worldview even as adults. This is why many adults don't feel like "adults". Their limiting beliefs are telling them that being an adult looks a certain way, i.e., the way they viewed adults as children.

We don't really get rid of our limiting beliefs. Instead, we get more information which improves our understanding. We challenge our assumptions. We ask ourselves better questions. We seek out new information and have new experiences. This is what gives us wisdom. Having more information gives us a wider perspective and changes how we interact with the world. We learn to see life as "both, and" instead of "either, or".

It's not a question of age. It's an ability to see things in a more nuanced way. Our limiting beliefs –assumptions– prevent us from having a deeper understanding of things.

Another automatic filter of our subconscious mind that we need to be aware of is a process called semiotics. Semiotics is the study of signs.[15] Our unconscious mind absorbs sensory input, and our subconscious mind translates it into symbols our conscious mind can understand.

For example, the first time you see a dog and someone tells you it is called a dog, your brain registers that data. Eventually, you learn to recognize the letters that form the word *dog*. Then you learn to connect that word (a symbol) to the image of the dog you saw (another symbol). Eventually, you will picture a dog just by hearing or seeing the word. Then, you develop even further as you learn to associate different images of dogs with the word *dog*. Then even further if you speak multiple languages! In that case, you will be able to associate multiple words with the image of different dogs! Isn't it fascinating?

Semiotics only works based on the information our subconscious mind has. Let's use relationships as an example. If I have a bad experience with a person who looks a certain way, my mind connects the pain of that experience to the way that person looks (and vice versa if we have a pleasurable experience). I am more likely to automatically react to someone who looks similar in a similar way.

We innately trust or do not trust people based on this process. This is essentially the internal process which creates bias. When my clients tell me that they don't feel safe with people, I know that's not entirely true. What they are saying is that they don't feel safe with specific types of people based on this process of image and word association. How we learn to associate a symbol, a person, a place, etc. stays with us unless we manually intercept the process.

Outrunning Your Emotions

These automatic processes are happening all the time without our intervention. They impact how we process our emotions and how we see the world. By being aware of these processes, we can use our conscious minds power to disrupt them and be more intentional about what information we consume and where we need to expand our perspective.

Pain Gets Our Attention

Pain doesn't feel good, but it gets our attention. When we know how to take control of the process, pain becomes useful. Pain is our body's way of letting us know that we need care, not a reason to panic.

One of my favourite quotes from Taoism is "pain is inevitable, but suffering is optional". Pain is a natural phenomenon. We don't have to waste our energy trying to never experience pain. It's not a good use of our energy anyway - trust me, I spent most of my life doing it with no success! Pain is going to happen. Suffering is a result of ignorance and confusion. When our body signals that we need something and our subconscious mind doesn't have the right information to correctly interpret it, this results in confusion. We either take actions that don't resolve our pain or we feel stuck not knowing what action to take.

I like to use the example of someone giving you the wrong directions to get somewhere. You take this information and put these directions into your GPS. You then follow the gps and take action based on the information you have been given, but you end up at the wrong place. This is going to leave you frustrated and confused. You might even drive around in circles for hours thinking you did something wrong when really you had the wrong information.

This is what we do when we don't understand our pain and haven't developed the ability to process our emotions. We blame ourselves. We tell ourselves there must be something wrong with us. No-you've just been given the wrong directions.

Pain is an indication that we have an unmet need. Suffering is what happens when we don't process our pain and therefore don't address our needs.

Dutch philosopher Baruch Spinoza's premise is that suffering will cease when understanding has been reached.[16] This has certainly been my experience, and I've seen it happen with my clients as well. As soon as we have clarity on what our emotions are and we begin to process them correctly, we end our suffering.

Due to being emotionally underdeveloped, most people have a lot of limiting beliefs and horrible semiotic associations to emotions. (We are going to debunk some of these misconceptions in Chapter 3). These automatic processes are controlling their lives. This leaves them without the correct information to make the right decisions or take the right actions. This ignorance leads to confusion and suffering and not only causes mental suffering, but physical suffering as well.

It's Not Always Depression

Disclaimer: I am not a medical doctor. The only body I am intimately familiar with is my own. I have made reference to relevant sources where I can, and I will be making statements in this section related to my own experience. None of this should be considered medical advice. Please speak to your healthcare provider regarding your specific circumstances.

Personally, when my body is in pain, I know it is trying to get my attention. I have found that if I pay attention, I will notice there are feelings and emotions that I am not processing. This build up of unprocessed emotions is called stress. "Stress is a feeling of emotional and physical tension."[17]

It's no secret that stress causes all kinds of issues in our bodies, especially chronic stress. The well-known book by Bessel van der Kolk, *The Body Keeps the Score,* speaks about how insecure attachment and traumatic experiences disconnect our body from our mind (i.e., psyche). This breakdown in the system prevents us from fully processing our emotions and keeps us stuck.

Suppressed emotions are definitely stressing our bodies out. Getting in touch with my emotions helped me get in touch with my physical body. For some people, it's the other way around. Either way, our emotions are linked to our bodies through our nervous systems. For over a decade, my body was abused in some way. My emotional pain manifested as physical pain that had no clear explanation. In medical terms, this is called a "somatizer" - people can turn negative psychology into physical pain.

Emotional and physical pain activates the same receptors in the brain (the anterior insula and the anterior cingulate cortex).[18] Our body chemistry is linked to our emotions and our thoughts through our nervous systems. These subconscious feelings and thoughts directly affect how we feel physically.

We think we can trick our bodies out of feeling, but even while our cognitive functions are distorted because we're high or drunk or distracted, our bodies are still holding on to the unprocessed emotions. The first time I got prescribed pain killers, I thought I had found the answer to life, but I had to keep getting high because the temporary relief would be met by an even more powerful wave of feeling, and I would often be anticipating that wave hitting me before my high was even finished.

A lot of people live with this chronic pain that cannot be attributed to a physical source because it actually stems from an emotional source. Our medical industrial complex is quick to prescribe medication to help us cope with our symptoms. The issue with emotional pain is that it is not easily proven. Thanks to the emotional healing I have gone through, I am free from medications, and when I experience strange physical symptoms, typically, listening to my body and addressing any unprocessed emotions helps me navigate it.

A great book that validated my work is by Hilary Hendle. *It's not Always Depression* and her change triangle method are great tools for helping people understand the connection between emotions and the body.[19] Her method is similar to my method - the Mighty Emotions Method (which you will learn in Part Two of this book). Both methods offer a framework to help you take control of the process when you become emotionally activated.

I have learned to check in with what I am feeling and what I am not allowing myself to feel when I am worn down, getting headaches, or any form of physical pain. I know that I hold a lot of tension in my muscles when I am suppressing discomfort. We can learn to recognize which emotions we are avoiding by becoming familiar with our body's signals.

Why We're Always Tired

Suppressing our emotions is physically demanding work. Not to mention how much work we give our bodies when we use things like drugs, consume food in excess, lack movement, etc.

Being tired may not be an emotion, but it is definitely how most people feel in our society. There is no question that we have many demands of life, but nothing is more exhausting than resisting our feelings. I had to ask *why* I was so tired all the time. (Turns out I'm anaemic and at the time of writing this, I also have a young child. Yes, I need to stay on top of my iron intake and sleep when the baby sleeps). But even when I am doing my best to take care of myself physically, if I am running from my emotions, no amount of sleep will help me feel restored. Not listening to my needs prevented me from seeing this for a long time.

Resistance to what we are feeling is the biggest way we leak our personal power. Power is energy. Emotions are energy. When we acknowledge the truth of what we are feeling, we actually gain some energy back. This energy gives us confidence to create lives that we love.

You'd be shocked at how much energy you would have if you just paid attention to your emotions and focused on getting your needs met. When we neglect ourselves physically and emotionally, it leads us to burnout. Living that way is not sustainable. We need our energy to tackle life's inevitable challenges.

When we don't process our emotions, our 'window of tolerance' is extremely short. We are quick to lose our temper or burst into tears at the slightest thing. Our window of tolerance determines how well we are able to function.[20] It's important that we take care of ourselves so we can widen this window of tolerance and increase our resilience. (We will explore this further in Part III.)

We can't stop life from happening. We need the fuel to navigate it. Our energy reserve is not limitless, and when we spend our energy wisely, we get more out of our lives. Spending all our energy trying not to feel or trying to control our external environments only steals energy from taking care of ourselves.

Now let's unpack all the misconceptions that keep us from processing our emotions and finding inner peace.

3

Mighty Misconceptions

Now that you know more about your emotions and how they work, let's talk about the most common misconceptions about emotions. Before we learn how to actually process our emotions, we need to unlearn some things. Remember that our minds are always filtering what we learn based on what we already know. If we want to start taking new action, we need to give our unconscious minds new information.

These are the ten most common misconceptions that I have come across, but I am sure there are more! The reason I am calling these misconceptions and not myths is because they are not entirely false; rather, they are incorrect based on faulty understanding. My intention for this chapter is to help you see the nuance that's typically missing for each of these misconceptions.

1. **"Your thoughts create your emotions."**

In Chapter One, we spoke about the nuance between emotions, feelings, and moods. Our emotions are our primal instincts that signal when our needs are not getting met. Our feelings are the meanings or interpretations we give to our experiences. Our moods are states of being that are manipulated by external events/outside sources.

Everything carries energy. Energy is sensory information that our unconscious layer of mind is constantly absorbing. We physically experience energy within our nervous systems. Every symbol (i.e. images, words, etc.) carries energy. This is why certain thoughts create sensations of uneasiness in our bodies while other thoughts create sensations of ease in our bodies. We physically feel a response to certain words or thoughts based on what we unconsciously associate it with.

Outrunning Your Emotions

We also have mood states[21], which refer to our overall worldview or state of mind in a particular moment. These are temporary and are mostly impacted by external sources and conditions. Many things can impact our moods. Art, colour, music, coffee, drugs, etc. Our bodies respond differently to these different forms of sensory input.

Not making the distinction between an emotion, a feeling, and a mood state is what causes confusion on whether "our thoughts create our feelings," aided by the fact that we use the words *emotions* and *feelings* interchangeably to describe our experiences. In the English language, a *feeling* is a noun while *to feel* is a verb. It describes the actual energy (i.e., sensations) we are experiencing.

While it is true that a different perspective can create a difference in how we physically feel, this is not the same as the biological responses we have when our survival is threatened and/or our needs are not being met. Our emotions are automatic, involuntary, primal responses. Our feelings are based on our subconscious understanding of what things mean. Simply put, feelings are controlled by thoughts, emotions are controlled by needs, and moods are controlled by external conditions.

We can experience emotions, feelings, and moods all at the same time. This is why we can oscillate between feeling good and feeling not so good. Feeling calm and feeling anxious. Feeling happy and feeling sad.

The reason it's so important to understand this is because we believe that if we change our thoughts, it will change our emotional experience. It can shift our mood. We can have better feelings, but our emotions only care that our needs get met. If we are seemingly doing all the external things and still feeling a void within ourselves, then we know that it's not about simply shifting our perspective - it's about getting our underlying needs met.

2. "Our emotions are caused by external events."

In Chapter Two, we discussed how we experience our emotions and how they are interconnected with our nervous systems and psyche (i.e., unconscious, subconscious and conscious layers of mind). We've discussed the nuance between emotions, feelings, and moods.

An external event can cause us to not have our needs met. It can lead to us developing limited beliefs and negative semiotic associations, but in and of itself, it is not what triggers our emotion. Understanding this nuance is important because when we believe that our emotions are dictated by external events, this leaves us believing we are powerless.

Outrunning Your Emotions

Additionally, this causes many people to believe that something is wrong with them when despite seemingly good circumstances they feel terrible.

You can feel awful even if your circumstances seem pleasant. You can feel peace and joy even in difficult circumstances. Why? Because our emotions are not directly connected to our external circumstances. Our feelings and moods are. We want to focus on getting our needs met and taking care of ourselves, not merely on getting temporary "happiness".

We also want to focus on the things that are within our control (i.e., how we process our emotions, feelings, etc.) When we understand how our internal systems work, we can take control of our lives regardless of our external circumstances.

Even under the worst conditions in human history, people have been resilient through these times because of their ability to take control of their internal world. We can control our perception (i.e., our feelings) regardless of our circumstances. In *Man's Search For Meaning*,[22] Viktor Frankl describes the positive effects of the men in the concentration camp supporting one another and their faith and connection to a Higher Power supporting them as well.

In times of slavery, the slaves would hold on to their customs and community to get them through it. Those were horrible conditions, but taking care of themselves and each other made all of the difference in the experience.

We don't have to be at the mercy of external circumstances when we understand the power we have to work with our emotions. Two people can share the same experience and feel completely differently. For example, if we both experience someone shouting at us, how it impacts us will depend on whether our needs are sufficiently met, what we have already experienced, and what we believe about ourselves and how the world works. I may live in fear of the world because I come from an unsafe home environment and I believe that other people are going to harm me. However, you may have come from a supportive environment where you learned to see yourself as worthy of respect. The impact of someone shouting at us is going to differ as a result of this.

This means that the external event (someone shouting at us) is not the direct cause of what we feel. We only look at the surface of how someone reacts and blame ourselves or think that something is wrong with us for being affected in a certain way. The truth is that we miss everything under the surface that is actually contributing to this. Don't focus on the external result - focus on the internal.

3. "Emotions are either positive or negative."

Here are synonyms for the word *positive*: constructive, practical, useful, helpful, optimistic. Here are synonyms for the word *negative*: pessimistic, defeatist, bleak, damaging, adverse. Words carry energy. The messages we absorb become our limiting beliefs. Are we taking a limited view of our emotions when we class them as negative? Are we deciding they don't add any value to our lives?

I know first-hand that my "negative emotions" are incredibly helpful. They help me see when I am out of alignment. They help me pay attention to where I need to take care of myself. They highlight the core needs that are missing and causing me to feel a void. Notice the words *challenging, uncomfortable, unpleasant* are not synonyms for the word *negative*. Our emotions can be tough, they can be demanding, they can be difficult, but not negative.

To call our emotions negative is to tell our brain to reject, deny, and refuse them. It limits our understanding of life. It keeps us in an internal war with ourselves that we can't win. This idea that certain emotions should be rejected is the main reason people remain stuck in suffering and don't get resolution from their pain.

Yes, some of our emotions are unpleasant to experience, but that does not make them a negative experience. Childbirth is one of the most positive experiences we can have as humans, but it doesn't mean that it feels pleasant.

More and more we are trying to encourage people to "feel their negative emotions," but the use of the word *itself* is the problem. That word sends a message to our brain that we should respond to our experience via distraction and avoidance. This leads us to remain emotionally underdeveloped. Becoming emotionally mature means learning to see the nuance in our experience and feel the full range of our emotions.

4. "Emotions cause bad behaviour."

Understanding childhood tantrums can help us with this misconception. A child (or adult) will throw a tantrum in response to the physical discomfort of not having a need met. They might be tired, hungry, or not feeling very well. Research shows "late talkers" are likely to exhibit more severe tantrums. When their language skills improve, their tantrums subside.

Outrunning Your Emotions

This is because behaviour is a primitive form of communication. It is a way of exchanging information. Being highly reactive is a sign that someone doesn't know how to process what they are experiencing or understand what they need.

Throwing a tantrum is a way of saying, "I have a need that isn't being met, but I don't fully understand it. Can you help me?" All those words are being said via whining, kicking, screaming, yelling, throwing, etc. The intensity of the tantrum will indicate how long that need hasn't been met. In other words, if we are immature in our understanding of the world, don't know how to process our emotions, and don't understand how to get our needs met, we are going to behave badly as a way of asking for help. Is a child wrong for communicating in the only way they know how that they need help?

In fact, tantrums don't stop at childhood. If we never learn to understand our emotions, or develop the language to describe them, even as adults we can behave in immature ways. There is a lot of judgment that we face due to the expectation that we "should" know certain things, by a certain age.

Due to our own limited beliefs about what is appropriate and inappropriate based on what we have been exposed to, we don't approach behaviour with curiosity. We don't ask, "What is this behaviour trying to communicate?"

This is not an excuse for poor behaviour. There are absolutely boundaries that we should establish for the protection and safety and overall health of our communities. However, when we make emotions the villain, we make semiotic associations in our minds that lead to us suppressing our own emotions.

I have had so many clients who suppress their anger because they associate anger itself with the aggressive behaviour of a parent. They don't want anger to cause them to act in a way that might hurt others. In our work together, I help them understand that the way their parent(s) behaved was not because of the anger itself but because their parent was unable to process their anger in a mature way. As they practise feeling anger, they realize that they can feel anger without being aggressive. The emotion was not a direct cause of their behaviour because they processed it in a healthy way.

Blaming emotions for a person's behaviour shows a limited understanding of how emotions work. When we allow ourselves to be curious, we realize there is more to it than meets the eye. If we want to feel safe with our emotions, we have to stop making them the villains.

5. "Our emotions aren't useful."

I hear this one a lot when people are talking about motivation and achieving goals. There is so much talk about emotions being the enemy of motivation.

The truth is that processing our emotions is the key to maintaining our motivation. Positive psychology explains that intrinsic motivation "is often experienced as more immediate and potent than extrinsic motivation".[23] We feel pleasurable emotions pursuing our goals because they fill our need for meaning and freedom.

But what about procrastination? Self-sabotage? Clearly, our emotions are to blame when we feel demotivated in pursuit of our goals, right? It is not our emotions to blame for this behaviour; its dissonance. Dissonance is a state we achieve when we are out of alignment, when we are not taking care of ourselves or getting our needs met.

Sometimes we are so focused on achieving a goal that we forget to take care of ourselves. We forget about investing in our relationships. We hustle and grind and fill our heads with the opinions and expectations of others that disconnect from our authentic selves. In this state of dissonance, we become anxious, demotivated, and frustrated.

As I have been writing this book, I have been struggling with this myself. I love my work so much, but I also have a family and physical sustenance needs and needs for fun and play that I tend to put on the back burner when I am highly motivated by something I love. In these cases, I expect my unpleasant emotions like anger and sadness to show up. I know they are red flags that my behaviour has caused too much imbalance, and I need to slow down and take better care of myself. When this happens, I listen to my emotions. I restructure my work schedule. I make plans to get my other needs met. I get back into alignment.

Our inner resistance is meant to force us to slow us down and take care of ourselves so we can have the energy to accomplish our dreams. I would say this makes our emotions very useful.

6. "Your emotions make you irrational and/or you're too sensitive."

It is really telling of the health of a society when statements like "you're too sensitive" or "you're too emotional" are insults. We use these terms to shame people who are clearly in need of support.

Outrunning Your Emotions

What makes someone more sensitive than others? In her book *The Highly Sensitive Person,* Dr. Elaine Aron, describes a trait called sensory processing sensitivity, a trait that approximately twenty percent of the population are said to have. [24] People who identify as highly sensitive are prone to being stressed more easily, need more downtime, and tend to be deep thinkers and feelers.

I myself identify with many of the descriptions of a highly sensitive person. I am very aware of when I am feeling physical discomfort, especially since I no longer use drugs and alcohol to suppress my nervous system response. When I first got clean, this meant that I was very easily triggered. I did not have a sense of internal safety because I mostly knew harm.

Lack of internal safety (i.e., psychological safety) determines how sensitive someone is to their external world. If you feel you are in danger, you are going to be more alert. Not feeling psychologically safe is due to the belief that your actions will lead to some form of harm (most likely because they did in the past). When we don't feel safe, we default to protective behaviours. These are commonly known as trauma responses.

There are six main protective behaviours (also known as trauma responses): fight, flight, flock, fawn, freeze, and focus. We all innately resort to these behaviours when we feel unsafe, either because we are physically unsafe or because of semiotics. We associate something about our present circumstances with harm we experienced in the past. As someone whose entire childhood, adolescence, and early adult life was filled with abuse and traumatic experiences, I can tell you that I have used all of these protective behaviours at one point in time. I will also use them in the future. There are times when these behaviours are necessary.

It doesn't take a severe traumatic experience to trigger a trauma response. Many people experience what is known as Complex Post-Traumatic Stress Disorder ("CPTSD").[25] It is a result of having your needs deprived for a prolonged period of time. It can result in similar behaviour to someone who has Post-Traumatic Stress Disorder ("PTSD") with the absence of a single traumatic event.

These are just some of the reasons people may seem irrational because they have a difficult time processing their emotions and feel unsafe in the world. There is no such thing as being too emotional. There is only being a human with your needs deprived for too long.

Outrunning Your Emotions

7. "You just need to calm down."

Have you ever tried deep breathing with adrenaline coursing through your body? Have you ever tried meditating while having a panic attack? Breathing is a wonderful tool to help people connect more deeply to themselves, but it is not always the appropriate response.

Emotional maturity is the ability to know what response is appropriate in a situation based on what needs aren't being met. Sometimes, as we already discussed, we need to fight or run for our lives. Those default behaviours or impulses can serve us in certain circumstances. Sometimes we need to stand up for ourselves and affirm our boundaries. Being calm is not always the appropriate response.

However, what is important is knowing how to self-regulate. As Andrea Bell from GoodTherapy.org succinctly put it, self-regulation is "the ability to control oneself, by oneself" (2016).[26] This is not about suppressing our emotions. It's about connecting to them.

Sometimes energy requires motion. Moving our bodies, taking action to get our needs met – that is how we are able to physiologically self-regulate and make better decisions from a more grounded place.

8. "You just need to grow up."

There are researchers who say we are not born with emotions, but that we develop them as our brains develop. I would agree with this theory except for the fact that I am not a walking brain. So much of the research that is done takes a very narrow view of what a human being is. Remember our emotions exist as part of a system. We can't understand them without understanding the entire system.

Remember Chapter One, when we discussed a baby's first cry? The idea is that because babies and young children only express a few emotions (sadness and disgust), they only *have* a few emotions and develop the rest later on. Of course children have the same emotions as everyone else! They are human beings. The research doesn't take the full picture into account, which is that children have a large percent of their needs met.

Adults are typically more focused on their children's needs than they are their own. They are proactive about making sure their children have food, safety, entertainment, and things to play with, connection with friends and relatives. We are constantly teaching them and helping them learn and explore. With their needs largely satisfied, they have little reason to experience other unpleasant emotions.

As they get older and are expected to be more independent, they start to have more unpleasant emotions because their needs aren't getting met. It's no wonder, because most adults don't realize what their core needs are. When I conduct a Needs Assessment with a client, it helps them see just how many of their core needs are not getting met and explains their overall dissatisfaction.

If you don't know what your needs are or how to understand your emotions, you are going to be pretty unhappy. All of us experience emotional suffering when we are not properly cared for. If we want people to "grow up" we have to teach them how to take care of themselves.

9. "Feelings aren't facts."

This statement is so controversial. Many people see it as empowering while others see it as dismissive. This is because people use the words *feelings* and *emotions* interchangeably. Feelings are not facts; emotions are. Feelings are subjective. They are the ways our subconscious mind translates the sensory information that our unconscious mind absorbs.

Feelings are the way we would *describe* the facts to someone. Our feelings are our perception of the world filtered through our subconscious (refer to Chapter Two where we discussed limiting beliefs and semiotics). It's important to challenge our thoughts and feelings by getting new information and widening our perspective.

Everyone's interpretation of their feelings is going to be different based on what they have experienced. But our emotions or instincts are all the same.

10. "_____ is an inappropriate emotion."

I cannot say this enough. *There is no such thing as an inappropriate emotion.* I hope by now I have illustrated all the reasons why this is the case. When we experience an emotion, it is because we have an unmet need. All our needs are valid. Therefore, all emotions are valid. Remember feelings, emotions, and moods are nuanced things. It serves us more to be curious toward our emotions rather than judgmental toward them.

Why We Have These Misconceptions

The reason I think the study of emotions is so incoherent is because most of the time it is being studied on external subjects. We look at how emotions and feelings manifest without really studying *why* they are manifesting. We focus on the external, which doesn't show us the whole picture.

I can speak so confidently to what I teach because I am the subject of my research. I am a human being before I am anything else. I came to understand emotions by observing them within myself. We are the only living species that can feel and analyze what is happening inside our bodies. We are the only ones who can hear what goes on in our heads. Of course, you can share it with others, but what they hear is being filtered through their own biases.

You won't have the same *feelings* about other people because you don't have the same lived experience as them. But we are all animals, and we all share emotions.

When we observe emotions only by viewing them in others, we don't get a full understanding of them. If we want to get good at controlling how we respond to our emotions, we need to take a holistic approach, which is exactly what you will learn how to do in Part 2 by learning how to find your power.

"Build a relationship with your emotions & you will build an amazing life."
-Jiselle Gilliard Jegousse

"Build a relationship with your emotions & you will build an amazing life."

—Iselle Gilliard Iegorisse

| PART TWO |

Finding Your Power

4

Our Personal Power

Let's start reclaiming your personal power. One of the first things we do in a twelve-step recovery program is to admit that we are powerless over our circumstances, and our lives are unmanageable. You might think this is a statement of despair and would make one feel discouraged, but, in fact, it has the opposite effect. Humility ultimately sets us free. We can actually begin healing because we admit that the way we have been trying to control our lives up until this point hasn't made our lives better, and we need help to do things differently.

The conventional belief is that personal power means having the ability to change your thoughts and behaviours in order to improve your life, but that is only partially true.

What isn't talked about enough is the fact that we don't control the automatic emotions, thoughts, or reactions we have to the events that happen in our lives. What we *do* control is the choice we make after those initial emotions, thoughts, and reactions occur. What we control is whether we are willing to review and analyze these emotions, thoughts, and behaviours and make a decision for the future rather than repeat on autopilot. We control what we do with our energy. *That* is using our personal power.

Power is energy, knowing what actions leave us energized and what actions leave us feeling drained and depleted. When we pay attention to our energy levels, we know which actions are aligned and which are causing more disharmony in our lives.

A great visual of this is the Personal Power grid which is adapted from the work of Cynthia Scott and Dennis Jaffe[27] (see Figure 1).

Outrunning Your Emotions

Act only on that which you can influence or control.	Can Control	Cannot Control
Take Action	*Mastery*	*Ceaseless Striving*
No Action	*Giving Up*	*Letting Go*

(Figure 1: Sample of the Personal Power Grid by Cynthia Scott and Dennis Jaffe)

This simple chart illustrates which action is worth investing our energy. When we take action on the things within our control, this empowers us. Over time we are able to improve our decisions and develop self-mastery. However, we also empower ourselves when we do not act on that which we cannot control. We don't put our focus and energy there. This is where we get support and collaborate with other people and/or use our faith/spirituality to get the results we could not get on our own.

What depletes our personal power is not taking action on the things that are within our control – i.e., we abdicate responsibility to someone else – it leaves us feeling powerless and hopeless. It is exhausting to continue taking action on the things we cannot control or influence. This leads to frustration and unhappiness.

The things we can control are the things we can create or produce. The things we cannot control are the things that our efforts cannot eliminate or change. If we did not create it and none of our efforts can make it go away, then we don't have control over it, and our attention and effort is better served elsewhere.

From the thoughts we choose to focus on to the behaviours we exhibit, anything we put effort into, spend time on, talk about, or physically do is taking action. Not taking action is about surrender.

There are two parts to surrendering. The first is making an honest admission, stating the facts of the situation. The second part is adapting to the facts. Rather than seeking to change them, we adjust to new conditions. We work with what life is giving us by focusing our efforts on the things we *can* change. How we respond to our emotions is one of these things.

How do you currently handle your emotions?

All of us have experienced some form of harm in our lives. When we did, we either had supportive resources to process and integrate our experience, or we didn't. When we don't have the support to process our emotions healthily, we develop a fear of our emotions. This drives us to react in a protective way whenever we have an emotional reaction.

Instead of processing them, we suppress or deny them, wallow in them, distract ourselves to avoid them, focus on blaming others for them, commiserate with those who share our pain, or become hyper vigilant and anxious trying to control everything around us.

I personally found myself reacting to my emotions in all of these ways. It's no coincidence that I felt completely powerless in my life. I would go through cycles of depression and feeling prey to everything and everyone in my life.

Most of us don't even want to face our thoughts or acknowledge our harmful behaviours because we don't know how to deal with the emotional discomfort that is driving them. As a result, our subconscious scripts drive our behaviours and create problems in our lives.

We may not be able to control life events or the emotions and feelings that present themselves, but whether or not we face our emotions and feelings is something we *can* control. Not taking the time to challenge these feelings, disempowers us.

Emotional Responsibility

We can only mature to the degree that we are willing to take responsibility for understanding our emotions. Not taking emotional responsibility looks like trying to change our external world in the hopes that it will make us feel better. It looks like attempting to control other people's behaviour in order to pacify ourselves.

Abdicating our emotional responsibility keeps us stuck. It does not serve us to neglect ourselves, which is exactly what we do when we ignore our internal alarm system (i.e., our emotions and feelings) which are always indicating when we have gone off course or run out of fuel.

Outrunning Your Emotions

We practise taking emotional responsibility by slowing down; even stopping altogether, to take stock of how we are experiencing the present moment.

Reflection Is Our Friend

When we give ourselves space to think deeply about our lives, it fuels us to make better choices. We react in measured ways because we take the time to analyze our experiences and determine the steps that lead us to take care of ourselves and have more harmony in our lives.

This is *not* the same thing as ruminating or overthinking. Processing is about taking something through a series of actions leading it to become something new as a result. When we overthink or ruminate we are simply cycling our thoughts rather than challenging, analyzing, and transforming them. When we are harbouring our emotions and feelings instead of resolving them.

The purpose of processing our emotions is to make decisions that bring more harmony into our lives. We are reflecting on past experiences to try and understand what caused disharmony, what did we need, and with this new awareness, what we are going to change moving forward?

We want to process our emotions so that we can become more emotionally developed. With maturity we can feel safe in the world no matter our circumstances. We mature as we gather more information and build a greater understanding of who we are and how life works. Remember, children aren't immature because of their age. They are immature because they haven't had full experiences, so they see life in a limited way.

As we gain life experience, we come to understand that there are many different elements at play. Life is nuanced, and there are very few one-size-fits-all ways of interpreting facts. Processing our emotions is about being intentional with the ways we interpret situations because we know it affects how we respond to situations and people in our lives.

You Were Born Knowing How To Do This

You already possess the ability to process your emotions. In fact, you do it unconsciously more than you realize because you were born able to do this. As children, we are instinctive. We haven't yet learned to suppress our emotional reactions. We don't think about what is appropriate for a situation. We let our emotions come to the surface. I am not suggesting that children handle their emotions well. I am simply illustrating that at one point in our lives, we were honest about how we felt.

As we grow and begin to suppress/control our emotions, our body still has to process them because they still exist. There are so many ways that our bodies instinctively release and process emotions without us realizing. For example, yawning and laughing are both forms of emotional release, when we go from one nervous system state to another. Crying is another form of emotional release that we typically attribute to sadness, but it is not connected to any single emotion. It is just another method our body uses to release excess emotional energy. This is why it feels so cathartic to have a good cry.

We also have the natural urge to move our bodies when there is a lot of emotion trying to travel through our nervous system. We want to run, dance, exercise, etc. Humming is another way we try to soothe naturally. All of these are healthy ways of regulating our nervous system and we might find we already do or have done without realizing.

We also all have the innate ability to reprogram our subconscious, meaning we have the ability to form our own conclusions and make intentional interpretations of facts. Any time you make a clear decision, you reprogram your subconscious. Have you ever changed your mind about something? I'm sure you can think of something that you have outgrown or came to see in a new way when you had more information presented to you.

Our minds are meant to work *for* us. They help us understand the world, envision the future, make decisions, solve problems, etc. They are incredibly powerful, and together with our bodies, shape our experience of life. When challenging things happen in life, it is up to us to use our personal power not to change the events, but to make sense of them so that we can take actions that benefit us.

Getting Aligned - The Mighty Emotions Method™

When I realized that by taking the following four steps (in the order they are laid out), I could process my emotions and experience resolution from my suffering, I knew I had found a tool that I would use for the rest of my life. This method gives you a framework for processing your emotions whether you are currently navigating a difficult situation or you have been holding on to certain emotions for some time. It is simple enough to do repeatedly (notice I said simple and not easy). I have gained so many tools over the years, but I realized that I needed something simpler. Something that instantly allowed me to regain control in challenging situations.

These four steps must be done in this specific order to be effective.

The four steps of the Mighty Emotions Method™:
1. Noticing
2. Honouring
3. Listening
4. Responding (aka Aligned Action)

Step One - Noticing

This step is where we notice our discomfort. We identify that we physically and mentally feel "off." We notice that we don't feel grounded or settled. Part of this step is healthy detachment from our emotions. Seeing our emotions as experiences we have, not identifying as them. We are *feeling* sadness, we are not sad. We may be *experiencing* anger, but we are not anger.

This step requires that we get radically honest with ourselves. If we are used to suppressing and/or denying our emotions, we may struggle with this step. Many times my clients will tell me that they don't know how they are feeling. They feel confused.

This is due to the fact that they may be looking for *one way* to describe their experience. The truth is that we typically feel many things at once. You're allowed to have many answers to this question. It's just about noticing that you are uncomfortable and that your emotions have been activated. This is also referred to as being emotionally charged.

We can look for clues in our thoughts and our behaviours to help us identify how we are feeling. Maybe we notice we are responding with protective behaviours (aka trauma responses). When this happens we know something from the past, some unresolved experience, has been triggered within us. Our body is reliving the emotions we never integrated.

What kind of thoughts are we having? Are they empowering or disempowering? We pause to notice what action we instinctively want to take. Are we reaching for something to soothe ourselves like drinking or scrolling on our phones? Are we trying to escape the discomfort in our bodies by ruminating and overthinking? None of this is observed with judgment. All of these are clues that there are underlying emotions to process. Before any processing can happen, we need to acknowledge our discomfort and be willing to face it.

Step Two - Honouring

The next step is where we begin to take action, and the first action we need to take is to allow ourselves to be human and have our feelings. Stop trying to fix ourselves or tell ourselves we *should* be feeling differently. Sitting with the discomfort for a moment instead of resisting it. Honouring our emotions is about becoming open to understanding what we are feeling/experiencing.

This is a powerful step because it trains our nervous system to be able to withstand dysregulation without numbing. It only works if we are fully present to the physical sensations we are having. Where do we feel energy in our bodies? Where do we feel pain? How fast or slow is our heart beating? What do we feel in our toes? We do this to bring our mind and body into the same moment (often the mind is somewhere else while the body is in the present).

If you've heard of a body scan meditation, this is essentially what we are doing. Become aware of any physical tension. It helps to close your eyes as you do this. Use earplugs if you need to, but the purpose of this is to be aware of how each emotion feels in your body so you can become familiar with it. The more you practise this when a big emotion comes up, the safer you will feel when it does. Creating safety is essential because our nervous system needs to be in an open and receptive state for any new ideas to be absorbed. You cannot change your thinking if your body is in a dysregulated state.

This step is all about honouring your humanity. This is the part where we stop judging ourselves for what we are feeling and just allow ourselves to feel. When we resist our emotions, we are stuck with them for much longer. When we honour them, they can flow through our bodies as energy and bring us back into harmony with ourselves and our world. This is the step where we allow whatever we are feeling to be okay. We welcome it no matter how uncomfortable, because we know it's there to teach us something. This is the step where we find our anchoring techniques so that when life throws us off course, we know how to bring ourselves back to centre.

We need to create space to honour our emotions each day. Whether something difficult happened that day or not, having a regular practice of slowing down, connecting to our body, and digesting the events of the day clears space for us to not unintentionally carry unresolved issues into the future. We create an intentional moment where we acknowledge our needs and our values. This is essential to building resilience. By meeting whatever emotion arises with love and appreciation, we equip ourselves with the power to heal even the most difficult of circumstances.

Step Three - Listening

Now that we have created safety in our nervous system, it's time to analyze and understand what our emotions are signalling to us. What are the facts? How have we interpreted the facts? Are there other ways of looking at our circumstances? What do we need?

Our emotions are information. They are always showing us what needs have to be addressed. Our feelings are always showing us what stories need to be examined. Processing our feelings means gaining a new perspective. If we didn't name our emotions and feelings in step one (which is okay), now is the time to get specific. (The Feelings and Emotions Wheel is a great tool for this and I have a video in the "Free Resources" tab on my website members.mightyemotions.com where I break down how you can use it.)

This step is about remembering the truth of why we are feeling uncomfortable. The stories in our head have us convinced that it is because something is wrong with us or wrong with other people. This isn't necessarily true. When we listen to our emotions, we see that they are not there to punish us. They are there to help us get the care that we need or to evolve/mature in some way.

Step Four - Responding (Aligned Action)

Most of the time we notice that we are uncomfortable and choose to act immediately. This can lead to regret and doesn't ultimately address the root cause of our experience. Without the first three steps, we are *reacting* to life rather than *responding*. The preceding steps allow us to pause and gain clarity before taking action. Once we are clear on which of our needs are missing and we've decided how we want to get those needs met in healthy ways, we take action. We show up. We do the work. We have not processed our emotions until we have taken action and responded differently. This is how we set a new subconscious standard moving forward.

Outrunning Your Emotions

For example, maybe you always wait for people to reach out to you to make plans, but you find yourself frustrated with the state of your relationships. After processing your emotions, you realize that your current behaviour is blocking you from receiving the connection that you need. So you decide to change your pattern and reach out to others more. Your friendships get stronger, your need for connection is met, and you feel more at peace in general.

We will know that we have taken aligned action when we feel empowered. Like we discussed with the Personal Power Grid, only by taking action on that which is within our control can we develop inner mastery and resilience. Even if we are processing the emotions of a really old experience, the purpose is to identify what we need, what our beliefs are, and how we are going to respond to life from the present moment onward. It is about seeing the bigger picture and realigning with reality so we can have more of the life we want.

What About Disassociation?

You may have heard of the term 'dissociation.' What this term means is that we disconnect from our bodies and the world around us, escaping through our minds. We experience this as a zoned-out state. We may feel like we are daydreaming or the world around us isn't real. This is a process that naturally occurs when we are experiencing too much too soon, without the tools to support ourselves through it.

There's too much information for our mind to process and we disassociate as a form of self-preservation. If we are in the middle of a challenging experience or an unsafe environment, it is not the time to process things - it is the time for coping skills. We don't help ourselves by overthinking, over-analysing and becoming obsessed with things beyond our control.

It's not about inflicting pain by returning to the same stories over and over. It's about recognizing when we are in a harmful pattern and need to do the things that are helpful to reconnect our minds with our bodies. If you find yourself disassociating, take a break. Distract yourself by focusing on something enjoyable for a little while. Rest. Connect with safe supports.

We don't want to stay in this state for too long because doing so prevents us from getting our needs met. It could be that you need to get external support to process the things you are experiencing because it feels like more than you are equipped for. Sometimes we go through things that really are overwhelming for us to process on our own. Spend more time in step two. Honour your emotions and reintegrate by returning your focus to the body.

A Note About Personal Responsibility

A lot of times I hear people describe personal responsibility in toxic ways. We're told that it's our "fault" if we feel a certain way and not the external situation to blame. Or we are encouraged to wallow in our feelings because the external circumstances are horrible. Both of these descriptions are disempowering.

Here's the truth: personal responsibility is making choices. It is the ability to honour what we are feeling and decide how we want to respond to it. It is a privilege to have such agency. How can we take care of ourselves when we have been wounded? How can we prioritize our well-being in the middle of a difficult situation? This can be as subtle as going for a walk in fresh air or having a glass of water or tea. What matters is that we think before we act.

There is no personal power without personal responsibility. Our ability to choose, act with intention is part of what separates us from other species. We listen to our intuition and instinct, but we reflect before we act. This doesn't mean we overthink it. It means we assess whether it is aligned with the outcomes that we want. Remember: our unconscious doesn't provide the instructions. It provides the information. Our *subconscious* filters that information through our past experiences, and the *conscious* is where we choose.

All of us have the power to pause before we respond. God gave us free will for a reason. We have autonomy and agency over whether or not we act. We are not happy being at the whims of whatever life throws at us; we want to have control, so it's important that we are clear about what we do and do not have control over. We need to ask ourselves, *what can I do within this situation, and who do I want to be?*

Outrunning Your Emotions

Disclaimer

In the coming chapters, I will be speaking of each core emotion individually. However, be aware that in reality our emotions are not neat; they do not appear one at a time. Often we experience a mix of core emotions and many feelings all at the same time. The reason I am speaking of them individually is so that you can detect elements of the emotions that are showing up and have a framework to help you get unstuck and take action. Building a relationship with each of our emotions individually builds a foundation for us to work from, but please be flexible with the information in the following chapters. Take what resonates and add your own wisdom to it.

5

Sadness

Sadness is often a companion to change. Our relationship to sadness begins the moment we are separated from the safety and familiarity of our mother's womb. With change there is loss. There is a natural recalibration period that must take place after a change in our circumstances, which sadness guides us through.

Sadness can be comforting as well as uncomfortable. Like all of our emotions, how we react to sadness is based on our early experiences. For some of us, we were rejected when we communicated our sadness so we learned to suppress it. For others, sadness earned us sympathy and validation and we use(d) it as a tool to get our needs met.

My own history with sadness was keeping it to myself. For a long time, this repressed sadness manifested as chronic illness. I would be in and out of doctors' offices with terrible pain for which all the tests were inconclusive. Not honouring our sadness has the power to create physical pain in our bodies.[28] I thought I was a "negative person" for a long time because I could never seem to be happy. The truth was there was such a lack of support and connection in my life because I didn't truly open up to anyone.

When I began to face my emotions, sadness was the first one I allowed myself to feel. It was a relief to stop lying to myself about the emotional pain I was in and just surrender to it. When I was done moving through the sadness, the heaviness I had been carrying lifted. I got clear on what was missing from my life and began taking action to get the support I needed.

Let's talk about how we heal our relationship with sadness.

Outrunning Your Emotions

How to Process Sadness

Step One: Noticing

We recognize sadness by the heaviness it carries. The weight of sadness is different depending on the intensity of it, but the essence of it is the same. Sadness wants us to slow down. Maybe we procrastinate or feel a lack of motivation. We may even feel stuck in some way or have no desire to move or take action.

Sadness leaves clues in our behaviours. We find ourselves seeking comfort, whether it is through comfort eating or taking a nap or reaching for something to numb ourselves. We may listen to melancholy music or desire to sleep more or rest more.

We can locate sadness by noticing how we feel in the center of our body. We may feel a tightness or heaviness in our chest or in our heart. Once we are aware that sadness is present, we can start to honour it.

Step Two: Honouring

Sit in a quiet place for a moment and notice how sadness physically feels. Put your hand on your chest and take long, deep breaths. It can help to speak to the emotion by saying things like, "I honour you," "I see you," or "It's okay that you are here."

Don't try to rush this process to get rid of the discomfort. Slow down with the sadness and give yourself a moment to be present with your body. Close your eyes and imagine you are floating on water. Imagine you are weightless. What does it feel like? Honouring your sadness means giving your body time to process this emotional energy. After the emotional charge is neutralised, you will feel more grounded and with a clearer mind that can understand what sadness is communicating to you.

*See Appendix A for list of ways to honour your emotions.

Step Three: Listening

Think about your current circumstances as objectively and factually as possible. What has changed for you recently? Where do you feel a disconnect in your life or relationships? What have you lost that was meaningful to you?

Sadness wants us to pay attention to where we feel disconnected from ourselves or others. Connection requires presence, vulnerability, and feedback. If we are not feeling seen, heard, or understood, our need for connection isn't being satisfied.

It also asks us to examine what we value. When we lose things that are important to us and we don't have support, it creates a void within us that needs to be filled. That void is letting us know that we need to prioritize our connections with ourselves and with others. We need to ask for help and be open to receiving it. Sadness lets us know that support is needed. We use this understanding to determine how we respond to our circumstances.

Step Four: Responding

A great way to respond to sadness is to build a Sadness Survival Kit. It will include your go-to actions and items that help self-soothe, get you various types of support, and restore your energy through different types of self-care. Here's how you build it:

Using the following tables, write down how you are going to tackle each part of the survival kit.

SOOTHE - Engage the senses

Sight	Create a soothing environment or get into a soothing environment like the forest or next to a body of water. Look around and notice the colours, textures, shapes, etc. in detail.
Sound	Listen to wind chimes, soothing sounds, or relaxing music.
Touch	Give yourself a hug, rub your arms or legs, get a massage, or use a massage tool.
Taste	Enjoy your favourite snack /comfort food. Drink some soothing tea.
Smell	Smell essential oils like lavender or light a candle that feels soothing.

SUPPORT – Lean on something outside of yourself

Mental	New ideas. Learn something. Refer to your favourite quotes or mantras when you need to shift your perspective
Emotional	Who can you share your emotional pain with that will witness you? Can you witness yourself by journalling or recording yourself sharing how you feel and responding to yourself?
Physical	Who can you rely on for physical touch/support?
Spiritual	What is your connection to the spiritual?

SELF-CARE - Where do you need to be rejuvenated? What kind of rest do you need?

7 Forms of Restoration	
Physical	Sleep, bath, etc.
Mental	Meditation, journalling, etc.
Emotional -	Emotional releasing techniques (shaking, dancing, humming, etc.)
Social -	Solo activity or spend time with people that fill you up
Sensory	Sensory deprivation (close your eyes, lower your gaze, put your middle fingers into your ears and tune out external light/sound)
Creative -	Make art, intuitive cooking, etc.
Spiritual -	Prayer, divination, nature, etc.

    By remembering these three Ss (Soothe, Support, Self-Care) when sadness shows up, you can be prepared and focus on getting support, taking care of yourself as best you can in the moment, and being clear on what is meaningful to you moving forward.

Outrunning Your Emotions

When Sadness Shows Up

To help illustrate what it looks like to process our emotions using the Mighty Emotions Method™, let's follow the story of Eva as she navigates a difficult breakup from her long-term partner Jake.

After three years of living together and five years of dating, Jake decided to break up with Eva. For over a year, they have been fighting all the time behind the scenes. There was always tension, so neither of them felt comfortable at home. They would always be in separate rooms of the apartment, and when they were together, they would be off in their own worlds. They went to therapy to try to make it work, but in the end, Jake packed up his belongings and left.

Eva is devastated. She thought they would get married. They tried starting a family, but it was stressful and ultimately unsuccessful. They have a small dog named Maggie who stays with Eva.

Everything in the apartment reminds her of Jake. She feels like the energy in the apartment is heavy. It doesn't feel like home anymore. She is thirty-five, unmarried with no children, and her partner has left her. She feels like a failure.

Eva feels so lonely now. She gets under the covers and cries for a bit. Her best friend keeps texting her, but she just wants to isolate from the world. Rather than calling people to come over right away, she lies in the silence and lets the sadness come to the surface. She doesn't fight it. She surrenders to her body. She gives herself a moment to feel the heaviness. She embraces that it is part of going through this change and transitioning from one version of her life to another.

After some time, she feels calmer, more present. She looks around the apartment. Everything looks the same, but it is all so different. She knows she needs to move forward with her life but isn't going to rush the process. Right now she needs to process her emotions and take care of herself. Breakups are hard.

She thinks about what hurts the most. She is sad that she doesn't have a family - a husband and children. She admits that she wants to have that. It means a lot to her to build a family of her own. She thought it was going to be with Jake because he was so family-oriented and she loved that about him. Moving forward, she knows this is a quality she is going to look for in a future partner. She is also going to start taking better care of her body and her hormones because she desires to have children.

Outrunning Your Emotions

She was under a lot of stress in her relationship, so she decides that moving forward she is going to be more intentional with taking time to rest and eat well.

She thinks about the holidays that she spent with Jake's family and how much she loved them. Having a big extended family is important to her, so, again, she decides this will be something she prioritizes moving forward.

Jake always used to play jazz in the apartment. She misses that, so she puts on some jazz music. Not because of him, but because she loves the way she feels listening to vintage jazz. It soothes her, so she plays it on the living room speakers and eats some dark chocolate on the couch. In the moment she feels at peace.

Now that she has spent some time reflecting and honouring her sadness, she calls her best friend and invites her to come over for dinner. Her friend comes over, and they order takeout. Eva lets her friend know that she appreciates her. They hug and catch up on the other things that are going on in their lives. Eva shares what she's been learning about herself and what her relationship taught her. She talks about her dreams for the future and all the changes she is going to make. They laugh and have a great time being present with each other. Eva notices she feels present and connected, something she hasn't felt for some time as she has been living in a state of self-abandonment. She's grateful for her home that feels safe now, her supportive friendships, and she's optimistic about her future.

6

Shame

What creates our identity? Without getting too philosophical, our identities are the characters we play in the world. All of us have different archetypes within us that are expressed in different areas of our lives. The way we are in our careers is different from how we are in leisure activities. The way we are as a child or sibling is different from a lover or parent. We're all so multidimensional and dynamic as human beings, and we develop new qualities as we grow and our surroundings change. Contrary to popular opinion, this does not make us inauthentic or in any way diminish our inherent value.

When we are bombarded with the opinions of others, it informs how we see ourselves. We learn that certain characteristics are villainous and others are virtuous. We learn to judge ourselves and others as a way of understanding where we belong in the world and what our value is. This is constantly evolving, but our perspectives don't automatically evolve with us. That's where shame comes in.

Shame is there to get us to notice the ways we judge and disrespect ourselves. It is a signal that we have forgotten our inherent worthiness. Our judgments and stories are inherited. As long as we are allowing the opinion of others to define us, we are going to be unhappy. In order to truly love myself, I needed to listen to shame. I had done a lot of work to forgive myself and accept myself, but I still carried so much shame because I knew how others perceived me and I still held on to those opinions. Once I began to understand my shame, I realized that I needed to form my own opinions and take responsibility for my self-image. I needed to define my identity and remember my worth.

Outrunning Your Emotions

Looking at the things that caused me to feel shame helped me identify where I wasn't allowing myself to change my mind or see things in a more expansive way. I was keeping myself in the boxes that others had put me in. The truth is that other people are always going to see us through their own stories. We don't need to change how others see us. We need to change how we see ourselves.

How to Process Shame

Step One: Noticing

Shame physically causes us to shrink ourselves. We may lower our eyes, cross our arms, or perform another self-pacifying behaviour. Physically, we feel shame in our gut. It's an uncomfortable "icky" feeling that we have trouble describing.

When shame is present, typically we want to avoid interactions with other people. If we do need to be in social settings, we may feel the need to perform and put on a mask around others which leaves us feeling social anxiety. We become hyper-focused on looking for cues that others approve of us.

Our first step is noticing how comfortable we are or are not when in the company of other people. This is when shame tends to get activated.

Step Two: Honouring

Honouring shame is about physically comforting ourselves. We can place our hands on our heart or our gut. Honouring shame is about showing ourselves unconditional love. We want to spend time connecting to ourselves instead of running.

By sitting quietly and wrapping our arms around ourselves, squeezing each shoulder, holding for a moment and then releasing. It is a way of tangibly expressing that we are holding and supporting ourselves through physical discomfort.

Step Three: Listening

Contrary to popular belief, we don't need to find our identity, we need to *define* it. Shame wants us to release the image others gave us and to get clear on who we have become and who we are becoming. It asks us to remember our value.

Outrunning Your Emotions

A natural form of trying to get our need for belonging met is trying to live up to the expectations of others. None of us want to be rejected or judged, but shame highlights where we are rejecting ourselves. We need to analyze our beliefs about who we are, the subjective interpretations we have picked up from others, and form our own opinions and aligned definitions.

What are the false narratives we have about ourselves? What are the beliefs that aren't serving us? Shame wants us to release all those heavy lies that make us squirm in order to reconnect to the truth of where we are today. What are the features, qualities, and traits that make up our <u>current</u> identity, and how do we define these on our terms?

Shame is a signal for us to remember that our value isn't dependent on the opinions of others. Opinions are subjective; both our opinions and the opinions of others. How we are looking at things is only one way of interpreting it. It is not *the only* way. We can always learn to see things differently.

Step Four: Responding
Building an identity profile will help us define ourselves based on our personal values. To do this, make a list of all the roles you currently have in your life. It might look something like this:
- Partner
- Parent
- Friend
- Sibling
- Employee
- Etc.

Think about all the different ways someone could define each role. Think about how you have been taught to see that role. What are the qualities that define someone who has that role. For example, next to "Partner," you might write, "Someone who is married."

Then, reflect on what your values are and how they can be brought into that role. For example, if honesty and quality time is something you value, you might write, "A good partner is someone who is honest in their relationship does their best to make time for their relationship."

Do this activity for any role you have that brings up shame for you. In a compassionate and empathetic way, define each role with the values that you wish to embody in it. This isn't about being a character of perfection; this is about identifying your value on your terms.

When you've finished, write your identity profile starting with the words, "I am the type of [sibling/friend/partner, etc.] who..." and complete the sentence with the new definitions you've written for each role. Then write examples of when you have lived up to this identity.

Shame wants you to take pride in yourself. Celebrate how far you've come. Remember the ways you have grown and stop looking at yourself through the lenses of others or of how you behaved in the past. Let go of those identity definitions so you can uncover the self-love that's already within you.

In Part Three we will speak more about self-love. This exercise of learning to form your own opinions is just a starting point that we will later build upon.

When Shame Shows Up

Eva is getting ready for her first social event since her breakup. It is her friend's birthday party, and everyone there is going to ask her about Jake. Only her best friend knows about the breakup. She has been too embarrassed to tell anyone else.

She sits on the edge of her bed and thinks about how she is going to respond to questions. How can she show up there single at thirty-five years old? Everyone is going to see her as a failure. She knows even if they don't say anything, they will be thinking it. Her and Jake looked like the perfect happy couple on social media. Everyone is going to think she's a fraud. Everyone is going to know she was faking her happiness, and they are going to lose respect for her.

She pulls out her phone to text her friend and say she can't come to the party, but instead she just holds the phone in her hand and stares at it. She feels like crying and hiding in her apartment. She doesn't want to face her friends. She knows they are going to judge her.

The discomfort in her gut gets her attention. *Shame* is trying to get her attention. She interrupts her mental spiral and puts her phone down. Rubbing her hands together to warm them up, she puts them skin-to-skin on her stomach.

"I'm sorry," she whispers to herself. She knows shame well enough by now to know that there are some stories she needs to release. She is

Outrunning Your Emotions

taking her situation personally and making it mean something about her that isn't true. She's also inventing stories in her friends' minds that have no basis in fact. She's projecting her own stories onto them. She pulls out her journal and decides to analyze the judgments causing her to spiral.

On a blank page, she draws a table. In the first column she writes, "What I am embarrassed by" and in the second column, "Why does this embarrass me?"

The first thing she looks at is her single status. Why can't she seem to keep a relationship? She feels like a failure and not a suitable partner. Clearly, Jake did not see her as worth staying with.

The next thing she feels ashamed of is how she made her relationship look perfect on her Instagram. She's embarrassed that she was dishonest and wearing a mask. She feels like a fraud and someone who doesn't deserve to be taken seriously. These are the stories her mind is telling her, not the truth.

Putting her journal down on the bed, she closes her eyes and puts her hands on her stomach again. She pauses and lets her body feel uncomfortable for a moment. After a few minutes of connecting to herself, she picks up her journal. Shame wants her to make her own opinion and definition of who she is. Her mind creates meaning.

Why does it have to mean she is a failure for being single and childless at thirty-five years old? She thinks back to the conversations she overheard her mother and aunts having about what makes a woman worthy. This taught her to define her worth by her relationship status.

On the next page in her journal, she writes, "What do *I* think about women who are thirty-five and single?"

"I think they deserve love and happiness. I think they are brave for having loved someone even if it didn't work out. I think they are good people. I think they are capable of having their dreams fulfilled. I think there are other relationships in their life, not just romantic ones that they can find their worth in."

She thinks about her friendships and how supportive and positive they have been. She begins to feel more empowered. She knows that she isn't broken because of this relationship not working out. She has a lot of evidence of being great in her other relationships. This breakup has only helped her be more honest with herself about what she wants out of her life and her relationships.

Outrunning Your Emotions

On the next line, she writes, "Why did I try to make things look perfect on social media?" She writes about how it was a distraction. She was unhappy and couldn't seem to make Jake happy. Again, she blames herself for that and thinks it means something about her worth. The validation she got from social media helped her convince herself, even temporarily, that everything was good even though it wasn't. She wasn't a fraud in the bigger picture of her life. She had been dishonest, but mostly to herself.

Putting down her journal again, Eva turns to face herself in the mirror. "You're a good person," she mouths to herself. She doesn't want to tie her worth to a romantic relationship anymore, and she doesn't want to try to escape her reality by creating a fake life on social media. She isn't going to be the type of person who pretends or avoids the truth. Besides, none of those things mean she is less valuable of a person in any way and shame was helping her to remember that. She closes her eyes for a minute and takes a deep breath. The shame has subsided.

She gets up and goes to her walk-in closet to pick out her outfit for the party. She grabs her favourite dress and does a mini twirl. She is becoming a new woman stepping into a new life. Sure she feels sad that things didn't work out with Jake, and keeping up appearances on social media was a bit juvenile, but she knows the type of woman that she is focused on becoming. Healed, strong, and proud of herself for not letting this situation define her.

She picks up her journal one more time and writes, "I am the type of woman who is kind to herself. I am the type of woman who knows what she deserves. I am the type of woman who is okay with criticism from others because their opinions belong to them. I am the type of woman who can show myself the same compassion that I would show to a friend. Thank you shame for showing me that I needed to remember who I am and to be a friend to myself."

Putting her journal back on her bedside table, she finishes getting ready to go to the party.

7

Guilt

There are two ways that guilt can show up in our lives: when we believe we have done something wrong by our standards, and when we believe we have done something wrong by someone else's standards. Any time we behave in a way that violates our values, we are going to experience guilt.

This is a really good thing because it forces us to act intentionally and correct our behaviour. However, we have to be mindful of when we are not guilty because of our actions, but guilty because of how others react to them. Sometimes we can cause harm by setting boundaries or prioritizing our needs. This doesn't mean we are wrong for doing so.

In these instances, guilt wants us to be clear about what we are responsible for and what we need to let others take responsibility for. No one likes to feel guilty, but it is important that we work to understand our guilt so we can make amends when necessary.

How to Process Guilt

Step One: Noticing

Guilt feels like a combination of sadness and shame. There's a heaviness to it, but also a discomfort that makes us want to shrink ourselves. When guilt shows up, we may become really defensive in our interactions. We may also be avoidant and externally behave in a state of denial.

Internally, we can find ourselves being really negative and critical of ourselves. We might beat ourselves up mentally, lecture and punish ourselves for "not doing better". We might feel the weight of the world on our shoulders and try to overcompensate in our actions.

Step Two: Honouring

In order to honour our guilt, we want to face it without being consumed by it. Similar to how we honoured sadness and shame, we want to slow down and connect to our bodies to honour our guilt. We can close our eyes and put our hands on our heart and focus on our heartbeat. We want to take a moment to show ourselves some compassion so we can become willing to look at our mistakes.

I find it helps to squeeze my hands together and force my mind to focus on the sensations in my hands rather than spiral with the judgments about my behaviour. I remind myself that guilt is a helpful emotion because I won't always do things perfectly, but I can learn to do things in a better way.

Step Three: Listening

Once we have relaxed our body, we get clear on where we need to make amends and forgive ourselves. What is the harm that we have caused? What are we going to do differently? A lot of the time, our minds immediately seek to justify why we did what we did. This is a form of avoiding responsibility. If guilt is showing up, then we don't need to find a justification; we need to make a decision. How do we want to behave?

This is about realigning our behaviour with our values and knowing when we need to prioritize certain values over others. Sometimes guilt can show up because we chose to prioritize our well-being over another person's desires. When this happens, it's about being honest with ourselves about what we do and do not need to take responsibility for.

Step Four: Responding

Making amends means changing our behaviour. How are we going to act differently moving forward? Getting clear on our values can help with this. The chart below is a useful guide for gaining clarity on where we need to amend our behaviour.

OUR VALUES

Remember that sometimes we will violate one value in an effort to prioritize another. Our work is to decide how we want to act in future similar situations.

Outrunning Your Emotions

What do I value?	What actions align with this value?	What actions do not align with this value?
Integrity	*I stay true to my word.*	*Lying*

We also may need to define our responsibilities if we are used to abandoning ourselves to please others.

OUR RESPONSIBILITIES

Guilt is our checks and balances, but when we are overly responsible, we are blaming ourselves for things beyond our responsibility and abandoning ourselves by compromising our well-being for the desires of others. Our job is to amend our behaviour when we act in ways that *we* are not proud of based on our standards, not just from our obligations.

Behaviour	My responsibility	NOT My Responsibility
Setting boundaries with my mother	*To be respectful and honest*	*To manage her emotions*

Guilt is about accepting ourselves as the flawed human beings that we are. We're imperfect, and occasionally we will misstep. Guilt lets us know when we have acted in a way that we are not proud of and we always have the choice to be more intentional moving forward.

When Guilt Shows Up

Eva picks up her phone for the third time in five minutes, but there is still no message from Brooke.

The party had started off great, but the later into the night it became and the more drinks she had, the messier it got.

She had no idea why she was drinking so much. Maybe she had been more nervous than she wanted to admit. She was so tired of keeping herself together all the time. She just wanted to let loose for once. It had been her first time out as a single woman and it felt terrifying, yet liberating.

Outrunning Your Emotions

She felt calm and confident walking into the party. At one point, someone asked, "Where's Jake?" and she calmly replied, "We broke up" with a half-smile and a slight shrug.

They were shocked. "But you looked so happy?"

"I know," Eva replied. "I really wanted us to be, but looking happy on social media didn't translate in real life, unfortunately. Learned my lesson there."

She could tell that they had more questions, but Sarah, the hostess and birthday girl, came in with a tray of drinks. "Let's have fun, friends!" She started passing out cocktails.

Eva had a great time chatting with everyone. She had worn her favourite dress and felt great to be out of her apartment having fun.

Awhile later, Joey came over to talk to her. He started asking her about her and Jake. Joey had a really comforting nature to him. He was her friend Katie's long-time boyfriend, but Eva always felt like he had a little crush on her.

"Where's Katie?" she asked him.

"She's home sick, but I had to come to bring the gift," he said. He gave her a sly smile, "I'm glad I did though."

Eva felt her cheeks flush. He really looked cute when he smiled.

"Eva, stop sitting around and come dance," said Brooke pulling her onto the dance floor. As they were dancing, Brooke leaned in and whispered, "What are you doing, E? Joey isn't single like you are."

Eva froze. By that point, she was pretty tipsy, and the words just spilled out. "Brooke, just because guys don't find you attractive doesn't mean you have to ruin other people's fun."

As soon as she says it, she regrets it. The look on Brooke's face is as if she wants to melt into the floor.

Brooke immediately rushed into the other room. Eva just stood there feeling awful. She went to get her coat to leave the party, and Joey followed her. "Let me take you home. I was leaving anyway."

She said nothing but let him guide her to the car. She knew her friends saw them leaving together. What were they going to say to Katie?

They pulled up in front of her apartment. She opened the door and felt Joey grab her arm. "Are you okay? You said nothing the entire way here. Do you want me to help you get upstairs?"

Outrunning Your Emotions

She pulled her arm away, opened the door, and got out. As she was closing the door, she leaned down and said, "Joey, go home to your girlfriend," before slamming the door and stumbling into her apartment building.

Now she's sitting on her bed hung over and still has no response from Brooke. She does have a text from Katie, though. "We need to talk," was all she said. Eva feels like a coward. What a disaster. She insulted one friend and flirted with another friend's boyfriend. She lies down on the bed with a frustrated sigh. Even though nothing happened she knows this isn't the standard she has for herself.

Closing her eyes, she tunes in to observe the discomfort in her body. She lets herself feel the suffocating feeling in her chest. She lets the tears flow. This is not the kind of friend she wants to be. She knows she has caused harm to her friends. She has belittled one friend and betrayed another. Not her finest moment.

She continues sitting there and thinks about how she would feel in her friend's shoes. She pictures the harm she caused. All she can do is wrap her arms around herself and give herself a hug. She knows that she needs to make amends, but she has to have compassion for herself first.

There is no excuse for her behaviour. The facts are that how she behaved does not align with her values. She knows she will need to face her friends, fully own up to what she did, and accept the consequences. She never wants to feel or behave this way again.

She picks up the phone and calls Katie. Katie tells her what she heard about her and Joey at the party. Eva doesn't try to defend herself. They were not actions worth defending. She tells Katie honestly that she is not proud of herself. Even though nothing happened, she knows she allowed herself to cross an invisible barrier, and she understands if Katie no longer trusts her.

Surprisingly, Katie opens up and says she knows that Joey isn't really happy in their relationship. After she got texts from their other friends at the party, she wanted to hear from Eva before having a conversation with him.

She thanked Eva for being honest. "Sorry things didn't work out with you and Jake. At our age, there's no point in staying in a relationship that you don't see lasting forever. I need to talk to Joey."

Eva hangs up the phone, and thinks about what Katie said.

Outrunning Your Emotions

Katie had been gracious to her, and she is thankful for that.

She thinks about Joey for a moment and feels bad for how the night ended. Should she call him? Is it her fault that he and Katie are on the rocks? She notices herself feeling responsible for his behaviour.

"No," she says to herself. He knew he had a girlfriend, and he took advantage of the situation. That is on him. She's glad that she didn't go any further. Honestly, if Brooke hadn't grabbed her to dance, who knows how the night would have ended. Brooke had done her a favour by snapping her back to reality.

Ping! She looks at the notification. It's Brooke.

"Now I know what you really think of me. I don't need any fake friends. Don't text me again."

Eva's heart sinks. She feels terrible. There is zero justification for hurting Brooke the way she did. It was a low blow to throw her insecurity in her face. She wants to text Brooke again really badly and own up to what she did, but she wants to respect her friend more. Brooke has set a boundary so she chooses to honour it.

Eva sits on the floor and cries. She cries for Brooke. She cries for the harm her comment caused. She is really disappointed in herself. Her guilt helps her decide to behave differently moving forward. She would think before she speaks. She needs to grow up. Even if someone insults her, she doesn't want to play tit-for-tat anymore. She did that in her relationship with Jake. It was incredibly immature and she's ready to do better.

Nothing can be done to change the past, but she is committed to changing the future. She sits down and writes a letter to Brooke saying everything in her heart. She folds the letter, puts it in an envelope, and puts it in her drawer. She can't control whether Brooke forgives her, but she has to forgive herself. She hopes to get a chance to make amends to Brooke. For now, she is going to release her guilt, learn from this experience and be a better friend moving forward.

8

Fear

Avoiding the things we fear can create a lot of chaos in our lives. It can make us falsely believe that we aren't capable of handling challenging moments. It can make us feel weak. Fear is a powerful emotion that forces us to pay attention to the potential consequences of our actions and decide what we are okay with.

Whether our fear is physical or psychological, it makes sense. Fear, like all of our emotions, is always appropriate and justified. There is *nothing wrong with fear*. It keeps us sharp. It exists to prepare us by making us more aware of potential consequences (the key word being *potential*). When we are mindful, we can make better decisions. Not processing our fear can make us *overly* cautious, which leads us to suppressing our actions.

When we experience horrible things that we don't process and resolve, it is natural for us to want to avoid experiencing that harm again. We protect ourselves through our trauma responses. The key isn't to eliminate the fear - it's to use the fear to gain clarity and get prepared. Fear is showing us what needs to be conquered.

How to Process Fear

Step One: Noticing

When we feel fear, there can be a surge of adrenaline and cortisol, causing us to panic or feel a sense of urgency. We may speed up and want to rush through our actions. Our heart starts beating faster. Our breathing becomes quicker and shorter, and we are unable to feel at ease in our bodies.

Outrunning Your Emotions

Fear causes us to naturally react through protective behaviours. We may also know these as trauma responses. If we find ourselves behaving in one of the following ways, we are likely dealing with fear.

1. Fight - we become defensive or aggressive
2. Flight - we want to hide and avoid a situation
3. Freeze - we feel paralyzed, confused, or indecisive
4. Fawn - we abandon ourselves and submit to the demands of others
5. Flock - we go along with the thinking of the group and match our behaviour to fit in with the crowds
6. Focus - we become obsessive and hyper-focused on one element of our circumstances

Note that we may respond to all of our emotions in one of these ways, not just when feeling fear.

Sometimes these protective behaviours are appropriate to our circumstances. All of these behaviours can signal to us that we are experiencing fear, and it is helpful to observe what we might be avoiding, denying, or running from.

Step Two: Honouring

When we notice that we are experiencing fear, we can honour it by moving our bodies. Unlike sadness and shame, fear wants us to move. The hormones that our bodies create need to be sweated or shaken out.

We can honour fear through exercise, going for a walk, or dancing. Shaking is a natural way that our body regulates after fear. If you've ever been so terrified from an experience that you found yourself literally trembling, this is your body's way of trying to regulate the nervous system. We can intentionally move the energy in our bodies and neutralize the fear enough to listen to what fear has to teach us.

Step Three: Listening

When our need for safety and power isn't being met, fear is going to show up. This is a moment for us to really pay attention & look at the decision that needs to be made. What are our options in the situation? What are the potential consequences or outcomes? We need to decide what we are willing to live with in the long term.

It helps to use our values in this situation and allow them to guide our actions. Which of the options we are faced with aligns the most with what we value? When we make value-based decisions, we make decisions

Outrunning Your Emotions

that we won't regret.

Use this series of questions to help you tackle fear:
PAYING ATTENTION
1) Get clear on the threat. What are you afraid of? Is it fear, or is it excitement? What is the threat to you?
2) Are you in a trauma response?
3) What beliefs (stories) are coming up for you?
4) What will it cost you to take action from your trauma response?

MAKING A DECISION AND TAKING ACTION
1) Review your options. What are the different ways you can respond to this threat/unwanted outcome? (Try to get it down to two options.)
2) What matters most in the grand scheme of your life? What would most contribute to your growth? Which of these choices is more aligned with what is most important to you?
3) What is ONE action you are going to take toward the choice you've made? When we take a step, the path is revealed.

Step Four: Responding

Now that we are clear on the most aligned action in that circumstance, we can take the next right step. Even if the discomfort isn't completely gone, we anchor ourselves in the conscious decision that we have made knowing it is for our highest good. Only by taking action can we collect new evidence. This changes how we understand the world, how we see ourselves and how we see others. When we do the courageous thing, we instill a sense of pride in ourselves and reinforce the idea that we are capable and we are safe. When we process our fear and take action, we reclaim our personal power.

When Fear Shows Up

With the holidays coming up, Eva is terrified of facing her family and being bombarded with questions about her current single status. She has always worked hard to get her mother's approval. She knows her mother has expectations for her life, and she's terrified to let her down by admitting that her relationship didn't work out. She also has never stood up to her mother or spoken up for herself. Her mother and her aunts can be really dominating and aggressive.

Outrunning Your Emotions

She knows she is going to be interrogated and criticized by her opinionated aunts. She really wants to just bail at the last minute. Even though she is thirty-five years old, being around her family in her childhood home makes her feel small and insecure.

Eva doesn't want to continue this pattern of fawning with her family. She wants to learn how to feel safe and stand up to them. She decides to work out to move the discomfort in her body. She puts on her favourite workout playlist and sweats out the anxious energy.

After she has her shower, she sits on her bed and reflects on going home to visit her family. She thinks about past holidays where she left feeling so shaken from her aunts interrogating her. They would always ask her when she was going to have a baby. She never told them about the failed attempts with Jake. She didn't feel comfortable defending herself, and they were relentless.

She really looks up to the women in her family, and their approval is important to her, but standing up for herself is more important right now. So what are her options? She can continue to do things to get their approval, even if it doesn't feel right to her, or she can be the adult that she is and stay true to how she feels.

She decides that she is going to learn how to be okay without their approval. She doesn't want to miss the family gathering because there are other family members who she hasn't seen in a while, and she loves her mom's cooking. Spending time with her cousins is more important to her than having to withstand a few questions or critical comments. Besides, even if she avoids this gathering, she can't avoid them forever!

She works to prepare some responses to things she thinks they will ask and practises them over and over until she feels comfortable saying it. The practice in the mirror gives her enough confidence to try it in the real world.

She thinks about the fact that she is ultimately the one who has to live her life and deal with the consequences. She thinks about the work she has done to overcome her shame and define her new single status in a positive way. She still feels a little anxious, but safer being clear on what matters to her and knowing that it is her choice to walk into the lion's den and no matter what, she will be okay.

9

Anger

There is something about just hearing the word *anger* that causes a visceral reaction in us. Anger has such a negative stigma, more so than our other emotions because we often judge how unprocessed anger is expressed. A lot of times people think they are expressing their emotions when really they are expressing their *feelings* and using them as excuses for harmful behaviour.

For a long time, I made excuses for the way I behaved when I was experiencing anger. I hurt many people as a result, including myself. I made the excuse that my anger needed to be expressed when the truth was I felt so powerless and was trying to be in control. I didn't want to take responsibility for processing my anger. I just wanted relief.

Of course my anger was justified. I was in a great deal of emotional pain due to my boundaries being violated and my needs being extremely neglected. Until I learned to process my anger in a healthy way, I continued to hold on to it and allow it to cloud my judgment. It greatly impacted my relationships because I couldn't connect with others so long as I was in a 'fight' trauma response.

If anger is showing up for us, it's really time for us to take care of ourselves.

How to Process Anger

Step One: Noticing

Anger literally creates heat in our bodies.[29] Our heart rate increases when we are angry and creates a rise in blood pressure and body temperature. We feel a surge of energy as hormones like adrenaline and cortisol are released, similar to fear. If we always suppress our anger, we can feel like our muscles are tense. We may cry as a way of our body releasing the emotions we are suppressing.

Anger can be very subtle. We can be really closed off or push people away, especially when we are trying to control and suppress our anger. It can also be intense and explosive, and we can feel out of control. We can yell or say harmful things. We may have an urge to cause someone harm or cause ourselves harm, and we might throw or slam or kick things in an attempt to get the anger out of our bodies.

Step Two: Honouring

Our anger isn't the issue. The issue is that we deny our anger or try to get rid of it at all costs. It is bringing us important information, and we need to give ourselves a moment to feel it.

We want to be fully present with our anger, noticing the sensations in our body. Similar to fear, we can honour our anger through movement. Walking, jumping, stomping, shaking, or running are all good ways to process anger. Humming is a good way if we are not able to move in the moment because the vibration helps to move the energy and neutralize it. If it's safe to do so, we can scream to release the anger.

Another great way to honour anger is to use a solid object like a table or a wall or a tree and push against it as hard as we can, imagining the energy flowing out of our hands and into the object. I don't advise that we do something to take the anger out on ourselves or someone else, but an inanimate object can support us as we shift from one nervous system state to another.

Step Three: Listening

Anger protects our limits, whether that is our mental, emotional, physical, and spiritual boundaries that need to be respected, or we have reached our limit of neglecting a core need. We can only go so long without getting our needs met before it impacts our survival. The disharmony or imbalance creates intense emotions of anger because our body and psyche are desperate for care. For example, if we go too long without eating, we can become angry and aggressive.

If our boundaries are violated, or we attempt to control others (which is a boundary violation), anger is going to show up. Our need for

Outrunning Your Emotions

safety isn't being met and anger wants us to do something about it.

Using the charts below, make a list of your boundaries in the present day. What are the things that make you uncomfortable? Write down how you can honour this boundary.

Boundary Type	How do I honour this boundary?
Emotional	*I allow myself to experience my honest emotions.*
Physical	*I choose what I am comfortable sharing and who I am comfortable closely interacting with.*
Time	*I honour my time commitments.*
Mental	*I am entitled to my opinions.*
Spiritual	*I have a spiritual practice that works for me.*

<u>**Boundary Violations**</u>

Boundary Type	Example of Violation
Emotional	*Someone trying to convince you to feel or not feel a certain way.*
Physical	*Someone takes something without asking.* *Someone makes us physically uncomfortable.* *Someone talks to us in a disrespectful way.*
Time	*Someone shows up late with no notice.*
Mental	*Someone trying to force you to think what they think.*
Spiritual	*Someone trying to force you to believe what they believe.*

Outrunning Your Emotions

Step Four: Responding

We need to respect our limits and decide what we will and will not tolerate. When we set a boundary, we need to enforce the boundary by taking care of ourselves.

Honouring Our Boundaries

Boundary Type	Example of Enforcement
Emotional	*Tune out the external and tune in to how you really feel. Allow others to have their emotions without trying to fix them.*
Physical	*Take physical space. Get support to put distance between yourself and the person causing harm.*
Time	*Decide how long you are willing to wait, and once the limit has been passed, leave or make other plans.*
Mental	*Be clear on what your opinion is. Allow yourself to have your own opinion. Allow others to have their own opinions.*
Spiritual	*Keep your spiritual practices personal to yourself. Do not try to force someone else to have the same practices.*

Our boundaries are how we protect our personal integrity and honour our limits. When our boundaries are violated and when we violate the boundaries of others, anger often shows up.

When Anger Shows Up

As soon as Eva opens the door, her mother rushes into the apartment and heads straight to the kitchen with several bags of groceries. It is Sunday afternoon, and she thought it was her Uber order being delivered.

"I knew the fridge would be empty," she hears her mother say from the kitchen.

Eva closes the front door and sighs.

As soon as her mother heard about the breakup, she rushed into rescue mode. She has started calling every day just to "check in" and make sure Eva is okay, as if the breakup has made her unable to function.

Outrunning Your Emotions

"Mom, I was planning to get groceries tomorrow after work, but thank you for bringing some over. Are you planning to stay for dinner?"

"What dinner? Do you think I'm going to bring you groceries *and* cook you dinner?"

Eva clenches her jaw, takes a breath, and then responds, "No, Mom, I just ordered some dinner because as you noticed, I have no groceries..."

"Ordered?" her mother cuts her off. "From where? You know I can't eat from just anywhere."

She gives Eva a disapproving look and begins putting the rest of the groceries away in the cupboards. Eva realizes her room door is open and walks over to close it before her mother has noticed the mess.

"Well, it's been nice seeing you, Mom. Say hi to Dad for me." She starts walking toward the front door. Her food would be arriving any minute. Maybe she could quickly swap her mom for a quiet dinner *alone*.

But her mother is busy washing the few dishes in the sink and doesn't answer her. The Uber driver knocks on the door, and Eva opens it.

"Eva?" asks the driver.

"Yes, thank you," she says with a smile.

"Well, aren't you handsome?" Her mother has appeared behind her and is smiling at the Uber-driver, who does happen to be quite handsome. "I hope my daughter gave you a good tip." She winks.

Eva can tell the driver is uncomfortable. She shimmies her way in front of her mother and mouths the words, "I'm so sorry" to him as she closes the door. He gives her a sympathetic smile and turns to head back down the stairs.

"Mom, thanks so much for washing up," she says, putting her food on the kitchen counter. "I really appreciate it. Say good night to Dad for me."

Her mom doesn't seem to hear her as she starts tidying up the living room. Eva feels warmth gather in her face. All her muscles tense, and she recognizes the anger coming on. Before she handles this in a way she will regret, she slips into the bathroom and runs the tap.

She splashes some water on her face. "Ughh." She punches the air. She starts jumping up and down to let the frustrated energy move. Years ago, she would have suppressed the anger until she exploded, but she knows now that she needs to move her body when it comes up. After jumping up and down a few times, she shakes, flailing her arms around her. A few minutes of that, and she starts to laugh. She always feels silly letting her anger out. She turns off the tap.

She needs to tell her mother to leave. She is violating Eva's boundaries. She is in her own home, and her mother has shown up unannounced and critical as always. She is uncomfortable and knows she has every right to be. She also needs to tell her mother that she is an adult and will take care of herself as she sees fit. For so many years, she would shrink around her mother, but she isn't a teenager anymore and this can't continue. Rather than seeing her mother as some menacing authority figure, she sees her as a woman. They are both adults, and although she would always be respectful, she has to also respect her own limits.

After two deep inhales and exhales, she leaves the bathroom and finds her mother sitting on the couch watching TV. "Mom, I love you, but I want a nice evening to myself. If you want us to spend time together, please call and give me notice next time. I appreciate you bringing me groceries. Let me know how much I owe you."

Her mother looks at her without saying a word. Eva feels the discomfort of setting this new dynamic, but she knows she has to teach her mother to respect her boundaries.

"Well, all right, then," her mother says slowly as she gets up from the couch. "Don't worry about paying me back. You're my daughter, and I want to make sure you're okay."

"I am," Eva says firmly and kindly. Her mother grabs her coat that she left draped on the kitchen island and drapes it over her arm. She heads toward the door, turning back for a moment as if to say something, and then changes her mind. "Okay, enjoy your night, my love."

"Thanks, Mom," Eva says, giving her a kiss on the cheek. "You too." With that, she closes the door.

She can tell her mother feels sad, but she respected Eva's boundaries, and that's all she could have asked for. Eva will call her tomorrow and invite her to dinner at their favourite restaurant. She is proud of herself for standing up to her mom for the first time and not making her mother's reaction her responsibility. She listened to her anger and honoured her boundaries. Now she really needs to eat.

10

Disgust

Disgust, as an emotion, refers to indignation. It is a symptom of entitlement and is natural to occur when we experience life not going our way. All of us create our own mental models of the world in order to feel safe. When these models are threatened because life inevitably does not live up to our standards, it triggers our need for control and certainty. We become attached to our ideas of what is and is not acceptable and subconsciously hold everyone/everything to these expectations. If we are not mindful of this, it can lead to disappointment and resentment.

We typically confuse disgust with anger and label it as irritation, annoyance or frustration. Disgust is what we experience when we are living in judgment. We can be impatient, unforgiving and self-righteous. In this state we aren't really seeing things for how they are because we are so fixated on how we think they should be.

Intolerance is having a narrow-minded perspective. It's rigid, inflexible and unforgiving. Healthy change requires imagination and expansive thinking. It doesn't happen if we are holding on to disgust and unwilling to forgive. Typically we believe we are disgusted with others, but disgust is an indication that we are not being transparent with ourselves. We will realize when processing disgust that we let ourselves down in some way: either by not being honest or not prioritizing our needs.

Judgment is natural and healthy. It is important to have opinions and preferences. It is okay to have standards and to disagree with other people, events or ideas. However, disgust is a visceral experience that indicates having gone beyond just disagreement. It shows up when we feel unsafe psychologically and when we don't process it, can keep us feeling disempowered in our lives.

We won't approve of everything in our world and our lives and we don't need to in order to find peace. We're allowed to be dissatisfied with people and circumstances. Knowing what our standards are and what we disagree with is important information. However, disgust shows us when there is more to look at under the surface. We need to check our attachment to certain ideas. We need to accept that life will challenge us. Other people aren't bound to our moral code. When we process our disgust, we expand our worldview, we forgive ourselves, we develop more realistic expectations and are better able to find healthy solutions to problematic situations.

How to Process Disgust

Step One: Noticing

Disgust can feel similar to fear or anger. Our heart rate can increase, we can contract our muscles and feel tense in our bodies. There can be a feeling of revulsion; wanting to crawl out of our skin. We may feel a strong need to retaliate or control our external circumstances. Our natural reaction to disgust is one of vengeance. We want to attack what appears unjust by our standards.

We can be hyper judgmental or critical of others or ourselves. We can be really defiant and adamant that things be done our way. We become uncooperative when we experience disgust because of the lack of psychological safety we feel when our reality doesn't match our expectations.

Step Two: Honouring

We honour disgust by letting ourselves feel frustrated. Imagine softening all the muscles in our body.

Finding ways of exercising physical surrender for a moment helps honour disgust and give our body a chance to regulate that energy. Usually it helps to lay on the floor, remaining completely still, close our eyes and let the floor hold you, completely relax your body.

If disgust is showing up when we aren't able to lay on the floor, it can help to close our eyes and imagine floating in water. Try to focus on how your body would feel if it were completely weightless. These exercises help to regulate and return us to a calm state so we can be open and receptive to finding solutions to our problems.

Step Three: Listening

Disgust wants us to get honest and transparent with ourselves. Whatever is bothering us on a surface level, isn't truly why disgust is showing up. It wants us to swap indignation with tolerance. We can look at what's really going on under the surface to release our attachment to the way we think things should be in order to address the reality of how things are.

We can practise surrender and humility by asking ourselves where we need to forgive ourselves for something or where we have been lying to ourselves or neglecting our needs. With radical self-honesty as our starting point, we can objectively look at which of our needs we wish was getting met at the moment? How can we adjust our expectations and/or our behaviours? How can we respond to the situation without trying to change it? What parts of our situation are within our control?

Step Four: Responding

Surrendering to the things we cannot control and putting our energy and focus toward getting our needs met is how we start taking care of ourselves.

Even in situations where our expectations aren't being met, we can still be safe. Even when we don't control what's happening, we always have the power to decide who we want to *be* in response to our circumstances. Return to your values. How do they impact how you meet life where you're at. (Check the appendix for a list of values).

Real life is going to challenge our expectations. Sometimes our needs will not be met due to obstacles outside of our control (which we talk about more in Part III). Disgust wants us to approach our circumstances with curiosity. Instead of fixating on the problem, we focus on what we can do differently in the future.

Lastly, if all else fails, use humour. Maybe we are taking life too seriously. Maybe we are taking things too personally. Find a way to laugh at some element of the situation. Humour can give us perspective. Approaching things lightly where possible can defuse the heaviness of a situation. When we can practice gentle detachment from our expectations, it helps us respond more easily to challenging circumstances, not be consumed by them.

Outrunning Your Emotions

When Disgust Shows Up

A few weeks after the breakup, Eva finds photos of Jake kissing another girl on social media. How dare he! She's disgusted. They broke up less than three months ago! How can he move on so quickly? Clearly, this is someone he had been seeing before. He cheated on her! She always knew he's an awful person. That picture brought so much back to the surface. The reality of her circumstances stares her in the face. Jake has moved on. Her present and future do not look the way she expected it to.

She begins pacing back and forth in her apartment full of disgust and outrage about what she saw. Little by little, she begins to slow down. Soon she is walking so slowly from one end of the room to the other it feels like things are in extreme slow motion. She lies on her bedroom floor and lets the ground hold her. She feels all her muscles relax.

Why does it disgust her so much to see Jake kissing another girl? She realizes she believes there are rules around breakups. At least, these are the standards she has set for herself. To her she needs to wait at least a year before dating again; otherwise, it is disrespectful to the relationship. Unknowingly, she has held Jake to these standards too and took his moving on personally. It is an immature way of seeing things. He's his own person who is allowed to live life by his own rules (even if she disagrees with them). She realizes she's still trying to control Jake and they aren't even together anymore!

It is time to reorient herself and adjust to a new reality. Life is different now, and she has to accept it and decide how she is going to respond to it.

Deep down, she feels envious of Jake's behaviour. She secretly wants to move on too, but doesn't feel like she has the same freedom. Why is she still restricting herself instead of being honest about what she wants? That's exactly what her disgust wants her to analyze.

She gets off the floor and sits down on the couch. Jake is within his right to move on. *There is no universal rule that he can't,* she thinks. *There is no universal rule that I can't.*

She finds his account and unfollows him. Eva sighs. She wishes him well. He has moved on, and she will eventually move on too, in her own time, but based on when it honestly feels right, not arbitrary rules she created because she's worried about people judging her. She realizes that she can be okay if things are different now.

Time to focus on herself and who she is going to become.

11

Alignment

What does alignment look like? It looks like being safe in our environment and our relationships. It looks like having a balance of meaningful work and leisurely play. It looks like being free to have an opinion and doing what feels best for us. It looks like knowing and liking ourselves, and having supportive, reciprocal relationships. It looks like knowing what's important to us and making it a priority.

Alignment is defined as the state of being calm, peaceful and untroubled; a state of serenity. It's not achieved by accident. We have to put in effort to create an aligned life (i.e. take aligned action). Most of us don't realize when we are in an aligned state because it feels mundane. We aren't accustomed to serenity.

Growing up in a world where we are constantly stimulated, we can feel uneasy when our nervous systems are in this state. It's not that we are sitting still and just being. We can be living very active lives and still be in a state of alignment. It is a state where we are in flow, there are no problems to solve, and we can just enjoy our present experience.

Alignment is only achieved in the present moment. It is in the here and now that we realize *all is well*. This doesn't mean that alignment is better than other states of being. It is just one of the realities available to us in our lives. There's a lot of talk in the spiritual community about higher states of being, and it can be confusing because you may think this means "better" states of being. In reality, all it means is that you have grown through the more difficult moments and emotions and achieved some relief or resolution.

This is why the positive emotions we feel after overcoming

challenges are so rewarding. It is an achievement and a feeling of deservingness. We respect ourselves and our journeys when we show up for them fully present. The person you meet on the other side of doing the challenging work of sitting with your discomfort, facing your internal narratives and making conscious decisions, is worth it. The power you feel having learned to take care of yourself and the wisdom you gain from getting to understand yourself more deeply is worth it.

There Are No Shortcuts to Alignment.

Achieving this emotional state requires intention and presence. It requires staying in your body instead of running from physical discomfort. I know running all too well. But running only leaves us disconnected from ourselves. When we run instead of show up, our lives become inharmonious and unmanageable.

We are responsible for how we respond to our circumstances. It is a process that can be quick but isn't instant. Alignment requires us giving ourselves space to grow. We mature by slowing down, taking the time to understand our emotions and giving ourselves grace and compassion through the process.

Restoring Ourselves to Wholeness

When I finally decided that I didn't want to lie to myself anymore, I didn't know where to start. I had tried so many conventional methods for healing, but I had been using those methods to find temporary emotional relief. Eventually, I chose to just face myself.

I sat on my bed, legs crossed, and got really present with my body. I stayed frozen like a statue. I didn't think about anything. I just focused fully on the electricity that was moving through my body. I noticed the tingling I felt in my limbs. I noticed the tightness I felt in my chest and throat. I just sat with it. I wanted to know what would happen if I embraced the discomfort instead of trying to escape it.

What happened shocked me. After what was probably only a few minutes, but felt like an eternity of crying and swaying, I felt calm. Not temporarily relieved – this was different. I felt safe. I felt okay. My mind felt clear. I started to wonder, what next? I wanted to understand sadness. Why is it something we experience? The answer didn't come to me right away, but I stayed with the question. Why do we feel sad? Slowly, I started observing patterns.

Outrunning Your Emotions

All the times I had been sad were moments of disconnection, moments where I felt apart from or moments where I felt a void of some kind. I thought about what the "void" meant and again noticed a pattern. That void is not being connected to the people and things that are meaningful to me, and when that absence of connection, I experience sadness.

I also realized by reflecting on my past behaviour that I was subconsciously already seeking connection and seeking to fill the void when sadness would show up. I didn't realize the essence of what I had been doing because it had been in unhealthy ways (i.e., seeking connection from the wrong people or through drugs and alcohol).

Then, I wondered, why the discomfort? The answer was obvious, to get our attention. Discomfort can't be dealt with in a passive way. It forces us to take some kind of action. So, each uncomfortable emotion was trying to force me to pay attention so that I could address what was missing - not in me, but in my life.

I slowly began to observe and question all my emotions. I noticed the underlying patterns that were present with all of them. I noticed the ways I would instinctively behave and realized that somewhere deep within my unconscious, I was naturally seeking to get my needs met. All of us are. We are always trying to get connection, safety, meaning, and freedom in whatever ways we know how. We really are doing the best we can with what we have.

So, I started to pay attention to how I could get those needs met in healthy ways, and my life got better. I *felt* better. Safer. Stronger. More resilient. Every time something difficult happened, I would move through this process of sitting with my physical discomfort and letting my body process the energy. I would wait till I felt grounded and clear, and then I would think about what unmet need the emotion was signalling. I would make a choice to get that need met in a healthy way, not always in the moment, but just making the decision and beginning to act toward it made a big difference.

As I began to be more proactive about getting my needs met, I started to feel immense love and gratitude and serenity. I lived in a state of alignment instead of a state of survival more often than not. I felt at ease with myself. I felt safe in my body. I felt present with my environment, connected to others, to myself and to God/Divine/Universe.

Outrunning Your Emotions

Trading Survival for Harmony

I began to notice that when I was living in a more aligned state, I had less negative thoughts to overcome. I saw things with more hope and optimism. The same problems existed in the world, but I felt safe. The way we interpret life is different when we are in a state of survival. Molehills become seemingly insurmountable mountains. We think innocent things mean horrible things. For example, when I wasn't processing my shame, I was incredibly sensitive to the comments of other people.

There is a myth out there that our minds are wired for negativity. This is false. Why would we be designed with a mind that wanted to be malicious toward us? Our minds are always working for us, just like our emotions. Our minds are there to interpret and analyze the events of our lives so that we can make choices that serve our needs. Just like we experience discomfort physically to get our attention, we experience negative thoughts to do the same. We don't have to believe these thoughts; we have to see them as a signal that we are out of alignment. That something in our lives isn't serving us.

This requires us to have deep empathy for ourselves. We must humble ourselves with the knowledge that sometimes we make terrible choices that we are never going to be proud of, but we get to make amends by choosing a new way to respond to circumstances. Our unconscious behaviours are not a true reflection of who we are. That is where forgiveness and understanding comes in.

This practice of owning up to our flawed humanity only makes us better humans. We recognize that making choices is what makes us powerful. Doing the things we don't always want to do because it is the character we want to have allows us to create identities we are proud of. We start to see life as a blank canvas, which can be frightening when we don't trust ourselves, but knowing how to process that fear guides us forward.

We cannot overcome past traumas that haunt us until we do this work. We cannot become resilient without being willing to do this work again and again as life challenges us. But again, I remind you that *it is worth it*. This is how we find our power.

How do I know? Because since I was a child, I had been dependent on drugs and alcohol to live, and today, I have been deliberately clean and sober for almost a decade (at the time of writing this book) with no desire to numb my emotions. I was a sex worker who experienced years of sexual

Outrunning Your Emotions

assault, and today, I am in a safe and healthy marriage to the most incredible, loving man. I thought I wasn't worthy of being a mother, and today, I am a mother to an incredible daughter. I have manifested a life that I never thought was possible on many levels, but more than anything, I know how serenity feels.

Understanding my emotions helped me heal. It helped me love myself and feel connected to my inherent worthiness. It helped me stop trying to fix myself and actually have compassion for myself and others. It helped me navigate conflict in relationships and be okay when certain ones had to end. It helped me stop living to please others just because I needed their validation to feel worthy. It helped me accept myself fully even the ugly parts. Looking at those parts led me to make better choices.

I did not just do somatic practices to achieve this state of being. I had to do the work of understanding my needs, my values, and my desires for life that helped me embody this sense of trust in life. Facing all my emotions with surrender helped me mature. It helped me accept that it's okay that things aren't always perfect. It's all part of being alive. Every time I choose to face my emotions and my circumstances with the goal of understanding them and not getting rid of them, I gain so much clarity and peace.

This is what it feels like to live in alignment: it feels like being at ease in the body, calm in the mind, and having command of our behaviours. Build a relationship with your emotions, and you will build an amazing life.

| PART THREE |

Loving Yourself

12

Relearning Self-Love

Your worthiness is not determined by others or subject to opinion. As humans, all of us are inherently worthy just because we exist. There is nothing to prove or earn. This is why when we attempt to earn love, we are left unfulfilled and disappointed. We can waste so much precious energy and time trying to convince others to see our value. We forget that just because we don't see something, it doesn't mean it doesn't exist. The sun is still there even on a cloudy day. Your value is indelible.

Unfortunately, many of us are taught the opposite of this and live our lives believing a lie. If our early experiences of life are of being mistreated or neglected, it can convince us that we aren't innately good. We become disconnected from ourselves and others which makes it harder to reintegrate after difficult experiences and to process uncomfortable emotions. This distorts our understanding of the world and leads us to create false concepts about what it means to be loveable.

Self-love is a regard for one's own well-being and happiness. It is knowing how valuable you are, what makes you unique and special. Knowing that you are deserving of your needs being met, even if your external world doesn't recognize this. It is not a reflection or creation of your mind (as some spiritual teachers may say). For someone to not recognize your worth, they must not be able to see their own worth. Our worth isn't individualized, it is something innately human.

I didn't realize for the longest time that the only prerequisite to loving myself was agreeing to it. We don't need everyone on the planet to agree. The reality is some people are incapable; they simply don't have the awareness. Regardless of this, what matters is that we accept the truth. If you need evidence of this truth, look at a baby. Just like a baby, who we believe is deserving of love for no other reason than its existence, you are also deserving of it the moment you are born and the 'mistakes' you make in life do not diminish this.

The Truth About Love

Love is our birth right. It belongs to everyone. However, what we often believe about love is confused with *being* loved. We think that how someone treats us is evidence of our value. The truth is that how someone treats us is driven by their perception (which is a byproduct of what they have experienced). It is not personal to us. This is a huge part of processing our feelings. Our feelings are the meanings we give our experiences, but we have to be mindful that we don't always have accurate information to interpret things correctly. We're not always seeing the full picture.

No one can see the inner world of anyone else. We don't know what has happened to someone or how they interpret the world. We can't allow the behaviour of others to cause us to reject and abandon ourselves.

You are entitled to respect, but you won't always be respected. You are entitled to compassion, but it won't always be shown to you. There is no guarantee that you will be treated the way you deserve to be treated. When this happens, it plants doubt in our minds, and we take it as evidence that we are unlovable. We learn to unlove ourselves.

When did you first fall out of love with yourself? Was it in your early school years where perhaps you were bullied and rejected for the first time? Or did it start early in your childhood where you felt like the black sheep of your family? Maybe you had to present yourself in a certain way in order to get your needs met, even if that meant lying to yourself about what you truly felt or thought?

Not loving ourselves keeps us out of alignment and creates a lot of suffering. We begin looking for love in the wrong places. We settle for temporary affection instead of true appreciation. We settle for being desired instead of truly valued. We think that love is something found outside of ourselves because we never learned to look within. As we continue to take actions that reinforce this false narrative, we diminish our self-esteem.

Losing Our Self-Esteem

Self-esteem comes down to how we perceive ourselves and what

Outrunning Your Emotions

we think it means to be who we are. We make associations between certain personality traits and the roles we are playing in our lives. A lot of the time, this is based on what others have told us or how we've interpreted other people's behaviour toward us. It is not a true reflection of who we are. This is why shame makes us uncomfortable because it highlights the incongruence between what we are thinking of ourselves and the truth of who we are. Shame brings all the thoughts that we have made agreements with to the surface so they can be released (agreements are the thoughts we have accepted as true whether they are true or not).

Not loving ourselves (i.e., not seeing our inherent value) will leave us with this negative self-image and low self-esteem. Based on this, our inner dialogue will be more cruel than kind. We will convince ourselves that we are more different from others than we actually are. We will become mind readers and assume everyone is also thinking negatively of us because our subconscious is constantly scanning our environments for evidence to support our beliefs, no matter how false they may be.

We become consumed and obsessed with controlling how others see us in the hopes that it will change what we believe. We don't realize that our inner distress is trying to get us to take the initiative to change what we think of ourselves. So, we learn to wear a mask and to perform in ways we think will allow us to earn love from others. While acting in certain ways may get us temporary validation, the price we pay is further disconnection from ourselves.

We become reliant on outside sources to form our opinions and have weak energetic boundaries, leaving us feeling chronically anxious and disempowered in our interactions. It can be exhausting to constantly be wearing a mask to make it seem like everything is okay. Lying to ourselves and trying to force compatibility with people who cannot meet our needs will never lead to inner peace, only greater internal conflict. We cannot simultaneously deny our honest emotions and hold ourselves in high esteem.

In our early development, we either learn to respect and admire ourselves or reject and criticize ourselves based on how others treated us. We rely on our caregivers to help us understand and fully embrace what it means to be human by modelling, mirroring, and assuring us as our awareness develops. We see how the people around us behave when interacting with each other and how they behave when interacting with us and tell ourselves stories about what these interactions mean. This is all a part of forming connections.

Outrunning Your Emotions

Connection is important and the quality of our relationships establishes the foundation for our self-esteem. Some connections end up being harmful. Rebuilding our self-esteem is a journey to restoring healthy connections in our lives.

A self-love journey typically refers to strategies for increasing our respect and admiration for ourselves. It is often approached from an external standpoint. "Do kind things for yourself." "Take yourself on a date." "Get a gratitude journal." All positive actions, but what is often missing from conventional advice is addressing the most obvious factor: we need to first honestly embrace ourselves.

Self-esteem isn't built by trying to become someone else or being free from fault. It comes from surrender. In Matt Khan's book, *Everything Is Here to Help You*[30], he says, "Throughout the first stage of surrender, we respect the gravity of our feelings, acknowledge each thought, belief, or conclusion as having a right to exist, and welcome each experience—no matter how surreal, one-sided, or distasteful it seems." Surrendering to the full range of our human experience is the first step to improving our self-esteem.

Stop Rejecting Your Humanity

There is nothing wrong with being a human. In spite of our imperfection, we have so much potential for greatness when we honestly accept our experiences. A constant focus on our flaws and fixing ourselves is in direct opposition to loving ourselves and does more harm than good. It is also not *necessary* for us to grow and change. We can achieve the most growth by treating ourselves with respect and loving kindness.

When we are connected to the understanding of the goodness and divinity that exists within us at all times, we stop trying to fix ourselves and start nurturing ourselves in order to bring this goodness to the surface of our lives more.

Policing ourselves is a common indication that we are rejecting our humanity. This doesn't mean being wild or inconsiderate of others. Self-governance is an important skill, and when we are loving toward ourselves, we choose to act in loving ways intrinsically. We don't need to rely on external instruction or coercion.

Many times we only approve of ourselves if we behave in certain ways. This isn't truly loving ourselves. Self-love cannot be based on our identity. Our identities are always shifting and being redefined.

Outrunning Your Emotions

Loving *who* we are isn't enough. It's about loving *what* we are, i.e., human.

Most of us are misinformed about what is just natural human behaviour. We have learned to see being human through the eyes of dysfunction and diagnosis. Every behaviour that feels uncomfortable gets labelled and stigmatised. Once this happens, we never explore or become curious about what led us to behave in such a way. It no longer becomes important to understand our patterns because we think we have found an answer, unaware of how incorrect it is.

We don't recognize our instincts and intuition because we have been conditioned to think and feel based on the instruction of others. Modifying our behaviours to be a part of the community is a natural way of seeking to get our need for connection met. However, sometimes we need to question whether or not we are in the right communities for us. Do others share our values? Do we feel safe interacting with them, or do we feel the need to betray ourselves?

We learn so much when we practise radical self-honesty. We start to notice subtle nuances in our thoughts and behaviour patterns. We notice when we react to things instinctively versus how we were taught to act or how we are expected to act. If a human isn't restricted to one way of being then we aren't limited in the experiences, we get to have. Spend some time observing other people, and you will notice each experience is nuanced. This means that we get to decide what is really aligned for us. There is no *one* way.

I know what it's like to be expected to behave in a way that doesn't consider your humanity. Throughout my childhood, I found difficulty being in community. I never seemed to really fit in anywhere because I would be very aware of where the group was incompatible with my values. For many years, before understanding my emotions, I believed that my discomfort in that setting was a sign that something was wrong with me, for not being able to fit the mould that seemed to come easily for others.

As I grew and interacted with people more and more in different communities, I realized that there were alternative ways of living, thinking, and feeling. I started to align with some of these alternative perspectives and the way I understood the world started to expand.

It became important for me to find groups where there was compassion and grace for individuality, while also embracing and encouraging shared values. This shared respect translates into self-respect, which builds self-esteem. When my community did not have a set expectation of who I needed to be outside of core values, I was safe to show up authentically and get my need for connection met.

We should be able to learn from one another, both from our mistakes and our triumphs. We should be able to come together to form a beautiful mosaic of the different ways we can contribute to our greater society. This is built upon familiarizing ourselves with our core human characteristics and not just our individual personality traits. Who we are as individuals will always change, but who we are as humans is consistent. When we expand our perspective and expectations of ourselves, we leave more room for self-love.

Can Love Truly Be Unconditional?

Unconditional love is only possible if we fully embrace ourselves. If we practise acknowledging our flaws and our fears and not making our mistakes mean that we are any less valuable. Then it will be easier to love others through their development as well.

Loving ourselves doesn't require a contract. The only terms and conditions are to release the unrealistic expectations we have of being human and allow ourselves to learn and grow. We can't have self-love until we first accept that there is no such thing as perfection when it comes to being human.

Living is a process of making decisions and being transformed as a result of life's consequences. We won't like everything we do in hindsight, but we don't need to be perfect to love ourselves. We may not like everything we feel, but we can face it and listen to what it asks us to change.

When we remember that at our core we are good, when we remember that being human is a constant process of figuring it out, we don't look at our shortcomings as moral failings. We see them as opportunities. We allow this to motivate us and energize us, or we remain in resistance.

Rejecting ourselves is active work. It is exhausting work. Avoidance requires so much of our energy. Trust me, as a recovering drug addict, I know all too well the damage that is caused when we try to escape ourselves rather than showing ourselves unconditional love.

Unconditional love takes bravery. It requires tolerance. It demands that we regulate our nervous system so that we are in an open and receptive state to seeing things differently. There is so much untapped wisdom within each of us. As Sydney Banks said, "Throughout time, human beings have experienced insights that spontaneously and completely changed their behaviour and their lives, bringing them happiness they previously had thought impossible."

It may require more effort in the short term to override the subconscious programming that has caused us to forget our worthiness, but we save ourselves a lot of unnecessary suffering in the long-term by doing the work. Always return to the truth.

Realizing Our Worth

Our worthiness is never compromised; only our perception of it is. We have to do the work to redefine what it means to be deserving. When we say things like, "I am not good enough," what we are really saying is that we don't believe we have the right to certain experiences. Nothing could be further from the truth. What have we been taught it requires to deserve goodness in our lives? Who taught us that we needed to meet a certain standard in other to be worthy of positive experiences?

I used to believe that I wasn't good enough to go to certain places or have certain experiences. I thought that it was only for white people or people of a different class. I didn't realize for a long time that I had a right to those experiences simply because I desired them. I was deserving of being in any environment that called to my heart. I was deserving of the experiences that I dreamed of.

One of my mentors, Amanda Frances, always says, "Our desires are divine guidance." We have to trust that we are meant for the things that call to our soul. Letting ourselves have amazing, fulfilling lives comes naturally when we do the work to process and integrate the feelings and emotions we experience. From this place, it becomes second nature to get our needs met. We set boundaries more easily because we don't tolerate mistreatment. We are more intentional about our surroundings and our interactions because we are clear on what is important.

Sometimes, we might find ourselves unclear or confused about what we truly desire because our desires conflict with what we have been taught. Learning to love whatever arises is the first step of wholeheartedly loving ourselves, being compassionate to our experience of pain, and respecting ourselves enough to know when we need to take a moment to pause instead of rushing to fix.

When we love ourselves, we don't question whether we deserve to live prosperous lives – we are certain that we do.

Outrunning Your Emotions

How do we embody this belief?

Having a thought that we are good and deserving of having our needs met isn't powerful unless we embody it. Thoughts are different from beliefs. Thoughts are ideas that we have absorbed unconsciously. Beliefs are the thoughts that we agree to. It is the accepting of an idea as a fact.

Not all of our thoughts create a visceral response, but our beliefs do. In *The Four Agreements*[31], Don Miguel Ruiz talks about the agreements we make with ourselves all the time. As we have thoughts, we subconsciously choose which to accept and which to reject. This creates a filter through which all other input needs to pass in our minds. We become more close-minded when we fail to realize that we always have the power to break these agreements, stop believing certain ideas, and choose to believe new ones. We just need to get our bodies on board.

We embody a belief it impacts how we react to situations in our life (remember how our layers of mind work). We can't just think we are loveable; we have to emotionally agree to that idea.

Unfortunately, if our nervous system is in a dysregulated state we can't embody new beliefs easily. This is why it's so important to let our bodies process what we are feeling.

We take inventory of the agreements we have made, i.e., the stories we have accepted that tell us we are not loveable. Once we are honest with ourselves about these stories, we have the power to reject them and replace them with beliefs that are true. Here is an exercise I encourage you to do to help with embodying this new belief.

Exercise: Write A Self-Love Statement

Start by writing at the top of a blank page: "I am valuable. I am good enough and I am deserving of having my needs met."

Then underneath, write: "Even if..." and list all the stories you have that try to tell you this statement of self-love isn't true.

Outrunning Your Emotions

Here's what my statement of self-love looks like:

I am valuable. I am good enough and I am deserving of having my needs met.
Even if...
...my biological parents couldn't love me.
...some of my opinions aren't accepted by the church.
...I haven't always done the right things or made the right decisions.
...I have hurt people that I love through my actions.
...I don't have all the answers, and I am still learning.
...I can't get my needs met in this moment.
...I don't know how I will get this need met.

Doing this exercise helps us remove the conditions that we have placed on our worthiness. None of the things I've listed can possibly diminish my worthiness and the purpose of this exercise is to remind myself of that and release shame. Loving myself means that I continue to remind myself and reinforce this self-love statement by acting aligned with the truth. Over time, the 'even if' list gets smaller, and you start approaching your life from a more empowered place.

"But will I become selfish?"

If you look up the word *selfish* in the dictionary, you find synonyms like *egotistical, narcissistic, self-centred*, etc. People who value being morally acceptable actively work to avoid such traits. If you are reading this book, then you are probably one of these people and don't want to be selfish.

The good news is that you don't need to be selfish to love yourself. Loving ourselves extends beyond just us. Loving ourselves is about embracing our humanity. There is a ripple effect when we live with this knowledge. It becomes easier for us to love others because we see them for the valuable and worthy beings that they are.

Loving ourselves makes us less selfish because truly loving ourselves is not about loving our ego. It is about the core belief that all humans, including ourselves, are worthy of love, respect, and having our core needs met. As we are more tolerant of ourselves, we are tolerant of others. As we are more forgiving of ourselves, we give others space to make amends and practise forgiving themselves.

Selfishness is a sign of *not loving* yourself. You cannot truly believe in your inherent worthiness, so you seek to overcompensate for this void in harmful ways. An overinflated sense of self comes from a lack mentality. When we truly love ourselves, it is from a space of abundance, from a place of being already enough. There is no space for selfishness.

Once you understand and accept that you *deserve* to have your needs met, you're ready to understand what these needs are, and to start taking care of yourself.

13

Our Core Needs

There is no personal development without self-care. We can't expect to be happy if we ignore our needs. Our needs are not just for our survival; they are essential to our growth. Self-care is about knowing what our needs are and honouring them in how we live our lives. Not out of obligation, but out of our love for ourselves and a desire to prosper. When we know we are deserving of care, it changes how we treat ourselves and how we allow others to treat us.

Throughout this book, I have referred to the connection between emotions and needs. The work of psychologist Marshall Rosenberg, the creator of "nonviolent communication[32]", helped me put together the pieces as I was learning to better understand emotions. Nonviolent communication is a practice to use in our interpersonal relationships with the aim of meeting the greater good for all involved. It is about learning how to minimize the harm we cause others and can also be applied to how we treat ourselves.

Whether or not our core needs are being met is the basis of everything that we feel. If our needs are being satisfied, we feel what is commonly referred to as "positive emotions". Likewise, if our core needs are not being satisfied, we feel what is commonly referred to as "negative emotions". It also skews our perception of things if our needs are not being satisfied, which contributes to the negative feelings we have about our situations and in our interactions with other people.

Expanding Our Window of Tolerance

When our needs are met, we tend to have a much different outlook on life. We are calmer and slower to react. We are more open-minded instead of avoidant and fearful. We are more gracious and understanding toward ourselves and others. Our window of tolerance is how much distress we have capacity for, what we are able to handle versus what leaves us feeling powerless.

A smaller window of tolerance means our patience is diminished and/or we are more easily triggered. We may have a lot more misunderstandings in our conversations and interactions. We may take things more personally and be more defensive. This is typically when we are labelled as "emotional" or "overly sensitive*. All of this depends on whether or not our needs have been deprived and for how long. Our behaviour is always driven by how we can get our needs met.

An emotional reaction is a way of communicating an unmet need. Just like babies cry or a toddler throws tantrums to communicate that they need care in some way, being highly reactive is a sign of distress.

Distress is extreme anxiety, sorrow, or pain. Distress is a signal meant to get our attention and force us to address our core needs. Our bodies are programmed to set off an internal alarm system (aka our emotions) when we are not in an optimal state of well-being. The longer we take to respond to this system, the more likely we are to shut down and experience dysfunction in our lives.

There are many coping mechanisms that can give us temporary relief from moments of distress, but if we want to avoid dysfunction (aka. burn out, depression, etc.), we need to focus on getting our needs met.

Whose fault is it?

We are born completely dependent on others for our survival and our well-being. As children, we are masters at communicating when we need something, even before we learn to speak. We scream and cry so our caregivers know that they need to help us. The more they understand what human needs are, the faster they can respond when we are in distress. Once they address our needs, we go back to being happy babies/children.

As we get older and more capable of doing things on our own, we become more responsible for our needs being met. This is part of our maturation. If we continue to expect our parents or someone else to meet all of our needs(and not just the needs of a healthy relationship dynamic), we can become resentful and our relationships may suffer which only further leaves us without connection. A vicious cycle.

Outrunning Your Emotions

Some of us did not have parents who tried to meet our needs, and so we became hyper-independent and self-sufficient to a fault. We focus on our basic survival needs, which we know are within our control, but our more intangible needs (sometimes called emotional needs) go unmet because we are unaware of them or unable to get them met on our own.

When our needs aren't being met, who is to blame? Is it our parents? Or society? Or are we the ones who are ultimately responsible? The answer is, of course, that it is a team effort. We cannot get our needs met completely on our own, even when we are no longer one hundred percent dependent on others for getting them met. We are social creatures by design. There are certain needs that require the contribution of others. Interdependence is the way we live healthy and fulfilling lives.

We won't always be aware when our needs aren't being fulfilled which is why thankfully, we have emotions. Emotional pain, aka unhappiness, is always the indication that one (or many) of our core needs aren't being met and when we understand this we can use our pain as a compass, guiding us to make better choices in our lives.

The first thing we need to do is know what our needs are. There are many frameworks for needs out there. The one that I have found to be the most supportive has been the nonviolent communication approach. It is built on the premise that all of us really only have four main needs: safety, freedom, meaning & connection. Described another way, we all have needs of the body, needs of the spirit, needs of the mind and needs of the heart.

There are tangible and measurable needs like the needs of the body, which we tend to focus on the most. Basic sustenance needs are prioritized in our lives. This may be enough to help us survive, but not necessarily thrive. The other core needs that we have are more intangible, but no less important. Needs of the mind, heart, and spirit cannot necessarily be seen, but they are essential to our overall fulfilment.

The Four Core Human Needs

The ultimate state of harmony and happiness is taking care of ourselves and letting ourselves be cared for.

It's time to better understand what our human needs are and how to nurture ourselves by getting them met.

Outrunning Your Emotions

Creating Safety

Needs of the body - Sustenance & Certainty

Our survival depends on us having basic safety and sustenance in our lives. Safety is about the protection of our physical and mental well-being. It is the foundation which allows us to focus on our other needs. Physical safety is about our environment, our external surroundings, but also our bodies. It is knowing that our environment (both tangible and intangible) is free from harm and our boundaries are not at risk of being violated. This frees our energy to be directed toward other priorities. (For a boundaries refresher, see the chapter on anger.)

We also have a need for psychological and mental safety. Because our perspective of the world is based on the information we consume, we need to be mindful that the sources we engage with are supportive, that the things the people around us are telling us and the styles in which they are communicating align with our greatest good.

Some of the ways we can create safety is by having structure and order in our lives. Rituals and routine can create safety for us. Having a framework can help just make decisions more easily instead of being overwhelmed (We do need to keep in mind that too much structure and rules can have the opposite effect).

Being familiar with our environment and having consistency helps us feel safe. We can also surround ourselves with people who are reliable, trustworthy, and predictable. People who respect us when we communicate or indicate our boundaries. People who share our values and who we can be honest and transparent with.

This also applies to our communities, small and large, in-person and virtual. It is important that where we can, we are intentional about the environments we put ourselves in and the people we surround ourselves with. We can choose where, why and how much time we spend engaging in those environments.

Our physical sustenance needs are also critical to our survival. This means being in good health, having food, shelter, clothing, water, etc. When we prioritize our physical health and try to get good sleep, regulate our hormones, eat nourishing foods, and move our bodies, we have a better emotional state as well. As adults, we are responsible for knowing what our bodies need and to make a deliberate effort to take care of our health so that we can give our bodies the best possible change against illness.

Outrunning Your Emotions

Of course, we also need to rely on other people for our sustenance needs. For our physical and mental health, seeking medical professionals, healing practitioners, therapists, coaches, mentors, etc. can give us ongoing support and keep us accountable to ourselves.

We rely on others to employ us or sustain us financially through our jobs, businesses, etc. Financial health is an important sustenance need because it is required to function within our society. Getting support to understand how to properly manage our money, how to invest and grow our wealth, and surrounding ourselves with people who are supportive and/or also aligned with these goals, all contributes to having our sustenance needs met.

When our safety and sustenance needs are lacking, we can expect to experience several uncomfortable emotions. Anger is one emotional signal that can show up. If you have ever been *hangry* after not eating for a long time, you will know this first-hand. Again, babies are great examples of how we can experience distress if we go too long without basic needs like food and being clean.

We may also experience anger, sadness and, at a worse level, despair, powerlessness, or hopelessness if our boundaries are being violated, especially consistently. This may be happening because we are dependent on another person who is unsafe or because we chronically abandon ourselves and put other people and their needs before our own. This is an indication that we need to prioritize or protect ourselves.

Fear is another emotion we may experience when our safety and sustenance needs are not being met. Not having certainty can leave us in a fight or flight mode. We may be unable to focus on anything else but the immediate moment because our survival depends on it. Chronic anxiety can also be an indication that we lack psychological safety and have a lot of feelings that need to be processed and integrated with support.

To be able to process our emotions, we first need a certain level of safety in our lives. We need a certain level of safety in our bodies. If we feel unfamiliar with our emotions, we will default to our trauma responses and either distract or deny, which won't allow us to find resolution or peace.

Reflection Questions:
- How can you create safety in your environment and your relationships?
- What makes you feel safe?
- What makes you feel unsafe?
- How well do you take care of your physical needs (i.e., your sleep, your eating habits, moving your body, etc.)

Homework

Pick one area of your life where you currently haven't been taking care of yourself and could benefit from more safety or greater sustenance. Decide how you are going to get that need met this week. If it's not possible to get the need met entirely, pick one small step that brings you closer to having that need met. Record how you feel at the beginning of the week and how you feel at the end of the week. Notice whether getting this need met had any effect on your overall well-being.

Becoming Sovereign
Needs of the Spirit - Freedom

Sovereignty is about being in control. As humans, we need a certain amount of control in our lives. Healthy agency is being free to make choices; free from coercion. We are individuals, and respecting the boundaries between ourselves and others keeps our relationships in a state of peace. Seeking to control others or to have power over others is often driven by a need for safety more than anything else.

Too much rigidity or restrictions stifles our need for freedom. The freedom to make mistakes that we can learn and grow from. The freedom to ask questions or share a different opinion. The freedom to govern ourselves and make our own decisions.

Being able to have our own opinions is something we fight for early on in our lives(even if we give our power away later on). This autonomy and self-capability leads to greater self-confidence and therefore higher self-esteem. We are entitled to have our own feelings, beliefs, outlooks, etc. without the threat of being dismissed or imposed upon by other people.

We can get our need for freedom met by asserting ourselves more, defining what our values are and forming our own opinions of things. We can decide where we end and other people begin. We don't try to control others and give everyone the space to exist in the way that's best for them. If their way doesn't align with ours, we are free to choose whether or not we engage.

Freedom is about spaciousness. Our need for freedom gets satisfied when other people give us space to discover ourselves, to change, to grow. Being receptive to our viewpoints without trying to convert us. Allowing us to govern ourselves and respecting our decisions.

Freedom is also about having space for leisure: not having to be productive every moment of the day. Having hobbies and activities that bring us joy. Having free time to reflect, be still and integrate. Having moments where we are free from responsibilities and obligations and we get to explore and be led by our desires. The freedom to have the things that make our hearts full.

When we discover what we enjoy by making time to engage in those activities, this helps us maintain alignment and harmony in our lives. Having fun can fuel us to be productive in other areas of our lives or at other times. Rest is productive. It is needed to help us replenish our energy so we can stay resilient.

When this need is missing, we experience anger, sadness, and sometimes disgust. Anger, if others are trying to restrict us or impose on our autonomy, if they are pushing us to agree with them or think like them. We may also feel anger if we are violating the boundaries of others and encroaching on the freedom they are entitled to.

Alongside this anger, we may sometimes feel disgusted that things are not meeting our expectations or preferences, particularly if we are restricted in some way by authority or dealing with things we cannot control or exert our influence over.

Sadness is also an emotional signal that our need for freedom is deprived in some way. If we are always working and not making time for fun or enjoyable experiences, this can cause us to feel disconnected from ourselves. If we are not sure what we enjoy and never have quality time with ourselves, then we can move through life feeling a void.

Outrunning Your Emotions

Reflection Questions:
- **When was the last time you did something fun?**
- **What are your hobbies? What do you enjoy doing in your free time?**
- **What brings you pleasure?**
- **What three things best depict who you are as an individual?**
- **What makes you unique?**
- **Where do you feel restricted in your life?**

Homework
Decide which area of your life currently feels the most restricted. What would it look like to have more freedom in this area? Decide how you are going to create more freedom in this area and take action over the next week. Record how you feel at the beginning of the week and how you feel at the end of the week. What did you notice after doing this exercise?

BONUS: Decide what activities bring you the most pleasure. Choose three activities and schedule them into your calendar to do in the coming weeks. Try to aim for a balance of eighty percent work, twenty percent fun each month.

Finding Fulfilment

Needs of the Mind - Meaning

Finding our purpose is about knowing what is most important to us in the grand scheme of life. When we are aligned with our values and living in integrity, our lives feel more meaningful.

There are many different paths to purpose. Some of us find purpose by being involved in certain causes and providing some form of service to others. Others find purpose by creating and contributing beauty to the world. Or some combination of all of these things. Regardless of how we execute our purpose, the core principle is the same: purpose is aimed at something greater than just us.

We are part of a collective. Our actions affect other people, just as their actions leave an impact on us. Even one small action in our life creates an invisible ripple effect that has the potential to change not just our lives, but the lives of others. We are interconnected. Knowing that what we are doing is leaving a positive impact on even one other person is how we get our need for meaning met. The things we do for others feel

Outrunning Your Emotions

more significant to us than the things we do for ourselves.

Having people and interests that we deeply care about motivates and energizes us. The pursuit of meaningful goals helps keeps things in perspective.

Staying connected to the future satisfies our need for meaning. When we have things to look forward to, it fuels us. All of us are going to become a different version of ourselves tomorrow than we are today and than we were yesterday. The difference is whether we become someone of our choosing. Part of this is striving to grow, learn, and improve. Thinking about who we want to be. Allowing ourselves to be challenged and not being afraid of our greatness. If everything is too easy or too hard, we become numb because our other needs are deprived as well.

Defining a "well-lived life" and actively pursuing it gives us meaning. When we are passive or settle in any area of our life, we are unhappy because we know there is untapped potential. Deep within each of us is the understanding that life is sacred and time is precious. What we want may look different for each of us, but each of us wants something.

Others can help us get our need for meaning met by encouraging us in the pursuit of higher goals. They can collaborate with us to dream and envision a different future. Having people cheer us on reminds us that we are not alone. We are part of a bigger collective.

We can also get others to lovingly challenge us at times, reminding us and mirroring to us what our values are. This contributes to increased self-awareness in us. Other people can help us identify our blind spots and collaborating with others in this way is the surest way to bring about change in our world.

Not having a sense of meaning or purpose in our lives can leave us demoralised and depressed. An existential crisis can cause us to experience emotions like sadness, guilt, and shame. Sadness is present when we are missing what is meaningful to us. It can signal that we need to re-evaluate our priorities and see what isn't being honoured in our lives.

We may also feel guilt about our actions or shame about who we are if we are not truly living up to our potential. If we are settling in life, it means that our need for meaning is not being satisfied. When we are not being challenged, or we are living very passively instead of honouring the things that are significant to us, we lose our energy aka our power. We can't ignore a lack of meaning in our lives. We will notice a void which we may seek to fill with things that are unhealthy for us.

Outrunning Your Emotions

Reflection Questions:
- What is truly important to you?
- What are your top five values at this stage of your life?
- In what areas of your life do you not feel like you are living up to your potential?
- In what areas of your life do you settle, and how does it feel?
- Where are you currently contributing to the greater community?
- How can you use your unique gifts and skills to make someone's life better?

Homework

Think about an area of your life that you feel the least fulfilled in. Think about how you are showing up in this area and what elements of it drain your energy? For example, if you choose your workplace, maybe by always having negative conversations with your co-workers, you feel emotionally drained each day. Maybe you feel drained by the tasks you do every day because they feel like a dead end and you don't see how they align with what's important to you.

Having identified all the ways you're left feeling drained in this area, choose an action to replace it with. For example, if your conversations with your co-workers are always negative, practice steering the conversations in more positive directions. If you feel drained by your tasks, look for ways you can align what you do with your values. If you are counting down the minutes until you log out for the day, create mini challenges that you can do each hour or couple of hours instead.

Pick the area of your life which feels the most draining and seek to create meaning there. This way you are creating harmony in the bigger picture.

Becoming Interdependent

Needs of the Heart - Connection

A personal connection, a community connection, and spiritual connection are all needed for us to feel true happiness. None of us are meant to be completely alone. We need to experience belonging. We need to have spaces and people that share a likeness to us in the areas that matter. Fostering connection, being fully present with other people and with ourselves helps us deepen our traits of empathy and compassion.

Outrunning Your Emotions

Our need for connection is typically highlighted when we are dependent on others in some area of our lives. The importance of this need is often minimized particularly when we become adults with more agency and autonomy. We live in a society that expects us to be okay without connection, so we crave it more than ever.

We can't get our need for connection met by ourselves. Even the connection we have with ourselves is built on the interactions we have with others and the imprints they leave on us. Our self-image is formed by the sensory input we absorb from our surroundings. We can't escape our need to associate with other humans. We can find a lot of comfort with animals and through a greater spiritual connection to nature, but we are still social creatures by design.

The secret to connection is presence. While our need for meaning is met when we connect to the future, connection – whether with ourselves, others, or a higher power of some kind – requires that we are fully in the present moment. We fully engage our senses and consciously take in our interactions and experiences.

When someone holds space for us and sits with us through a difficult time or when we exchange our perspectives with another person, this helps us bond and form ties that give us greater clarity and peace. Other people also help us connect to ourselves by reminding us of our strengths and our gifts; things we may forget about or fail to see.

We are always acting as mirrors for one another. If we spend too much time alone or online, it skews our perception of reality. It is through interacting with the outside world that we find truth. A common phrase coined by motivational speaker Jim Rohn is "You are the average of the five people you spend the most time with." With the wrong people around us, it can leave us with many false ideas about ourselves and the world which keep us from flourishing.

As human beings, we also have a core need to orient ourselves toward some sort of higher power. Having some sort of spiritual connection is more important than we realize. It does not have to be through religion. For many tribal and indigenous peoples, it was through nature and storytelling. What's important is that we have a connection to a shared culture or a shared history. Even if our spiritual connection is personal to us, it is another form of being connected to the bigger picture and having a fully integrated mind, body, and psyche.

Disconnection causes us to feel numb or disassociated. Sadness is the greatest indication that our need for connection is being deprived, but we may also feel shame from being disconnected from ourselves. Processing this shame and sadness can reintegrate all the fragmented parts of us and we are restored to wholeness.

Reflection Questions:
- **When do you feel most connected to yourself?**
- **When do you feel most connected to others?**
- **Do you have a connection to a higher power or a spiritual connection of some sort?**
- **What communities do you belong to?**
- **In what ways do you practice being present?**

Homework

Practice engaging all your senses in your interactions this week. Whether you are spending time alone or with others this week, notice the sights, sounds, smells, and sensations. Try to mentally record this information. Then later, reflect on how you felt in the interaction when you were being fully present.

Spend some time reflecting on the vastness of life. Think about the interconnectedness of everything on the planet. Watch documentaries on nature and spend time outside at night looking at the moon and stars. Write about what you think holds this all together. Maybe it's a deity of some kind. Maybe it's just energy or something more scientific. Think about the events in your life where you had no input, but things worked out favourably. The lucky moments. The things that somehow just came together no matter how big or small they may have been. Write about how you feel about these moments. They have miraculously contributed to where you are now. This exercise is not about making you believe in anything specific; it's simply about helping you put things into perspective.

Take a Needs Assessment

A needs assessment is a quick scan of each of these core needs, particularly when we are struggling emotionally, to see where we are most deprived and identify what actions are required to get us back on track.

Start by using the Core Need Wheel in Appendix B to identify what percentage of your core needs are currently not being met. Then, do the Needs List exercise below.

Outrunning Your Emotions

EXERCISE: Needs List Exercise

Now that you've assessed how much (or how little) your needs are being met, it's time to reflect on *how* your needs are being met. There are healthy and unhealthy ways of getting our needs met. Use the following chart to help you get clear on what's really the driving force behind your actions (i.e., which need are these actions trying to meet). Identify alternative actions that are more aligned with your values.

Current Actions	Needs	Values	Future Actions
Constantly making plans to go out because I don't want to feel loneliness	Safety Connection	Self-care Self-respect	To get safety: process my sadness instead of running from it To get connection: quality time with myself

    What this exercise allows you to do is prepare yourself to *respond* differently. In the example above we can see our pattern for avoiding being alone with ourselves because we might feel really unsafe with the emotions that show up. We can identify our four core needs which may not be getting met (use The Expanded Needs List in the Appendix). Then we identify what we actually value because we want to take this into our decision-making for our future actions. If I value self-care and self-respect, I am not going to be comfortable with my current actions.

    An action that would be more aligned with my values and would also get my needs met would be to process my emotions and find ways of making time by myself quality moments (i.e., taking myself on a date, creating a comfy environment in my home, etc.).

    The formula to taking aligned actions is: what do I need? + what are my values? This exercise is meant to empower you by highlighting your patterns so you can have the information you need to make decisions that *feel better*. If you need further clarity, feel free to use the Values List in the appendix section.

We Are Always Going to Get Our Needs Met

Having our needs met is key to our survival, so we are always going to subconsciously be seeking ways and means to fill the void. This is why It is important to be mindful and aware of what our emotions and behaviour are communicating to see us. It is our subconscious mind's job to get us to take action in service of our needs, but this typically through short term validation and/or instant gratification.

When we meet our needs unconsciously, it can be more harmful for us because we are focused on the immediate fulfilment rather than addressing the root cause of our pain/discomfort. We can also feel limited in getting our needs met because we are so used to one way that we don't realize there are many potential healthy avenues for us to take. In order to be open to the opportunity always around us, we need some awareness of what it looks like to have our needs satisfied in different ways.

Here are some healthy actions we can take to get each of our core needs met:

Safety	Meaning
<ul><li>Trustworthy relationships</li><li>Having systems of organisation</li><li>Consistency</li><li>Getting sufficient/quality sleep</li><li>Moving your body</li></ul>	<ul><li>Creating new things</li><li>Feeling competent and capable</li><li>Being honest with ourselves and others</li><li>Having a mission</li><li>Positively contributing to someone's life</li><li>Learning interesting things</li></ul>
Freedom	Connection
<ul><li>Having options/ability to make own choices</li><li>Being a state of ease</li><li>Free from obligation</li><li>Hysterically laughing</li><li>Following your desires</li></ul>	<ul><li>Shared vulnerability/intimacy</li><li>Taking care of someone/being cared for</li><li>Belonging to a community</li><li>Attention and validation from safe sources</li><li>Being empathetic to oneself and others</li></ul>

Figure 2. Table of healthy ways of having needs met

Outrunning Your Emotions

This list is just meant to be a starting point and is absolutely not exhaustive. I am sure you can think of other ways to get your needs met than what I have listed here.

What matters is taking action. Sometimes one action can help us get several needs met. For example, a fun night out with supportive friends can satisfy our needs for safety, connection, and freedom, while being part of a volunteer group for a cause that matters to us can satisfy our needs for connection and meaning.

It's also not fair to expect one practice or one person to be the source of satisfying all our needs. We need to understand alternative means of taking care of ourselves in order to build a life that supports us. It also means we can adapt quickly if we need to as things change.

Let's be honest, it can be difficult to readjust and transition from one source of getting our needs met to another. When we feel safe with a familiar method or person, we can become too dependent on it and sabotage getting our other needs met as a result. Living requires that we remain solution-oriented. The ultimate source of power is our personal power to take care of ourselves. Even just by taking small steps toward getting our needs met, we are headed in the right direction, and it has a positive impact on our mental, physical, and emotional health.

Every living thing needs safety, freedom, meaning, and connection. The quality of our lives is determined by whether or not these needs are fulfilled.

Exercise: Emotional Survival Kit

Using Figure 2 as a starting point, create a similar chart and list all the ways in which you can get each of these categories of needs met in your life. I call this the *Emotional Survival Kit* because you want to keep this list handy for when you are struggling to remind yourself of ways that you can take care of yourself. Use this list after moving through Steps 1 and 2 of the Mighty Emotions Method ™ in order to not just find relief from your emotional suffering, but resolution.

Needs Are Not A Nice-to-Have

Our core needs are requirements for happy lives. Without them being satisfied, we will constantly be living in a heightened emotional state, which over time can cause serious physical and mental issues. Treat your needs as important. Regularly conduct needs assessments when you

Outrunning Your Emotions

are particularly anxious or uneasy and notice the difference in how you feel as you start to nurture yourself.

128

14

Letting Life Be Life

Living is about having experiences. Some experiences we will like, others we won't. At any given time, life can feel difficult because it is. Sometimes we encounter obstacles that prevent us from fulfilling our needs. The impact of this should be acknowledged. Everything isn't always our fault or our responsibility. We are constantly co-creating our lived experiences energetically and physically.

Even when we are doing our best to live intentionally, life won't always go our way. This is why truly becoming resilient requires that we show ourselves compassion. Resilience is not that we never get knocked down. It is our ability to continue to get back up each time.

Self-compassion is the key to overcoming past traumas and being able to face whatever life throws our way. No matter how much work we do toward loving ourselves and taking better care of ourselves, the reality is that sometimes life gets in the way. What matters most is how we handle the moments in life that are outside of our control. We are never going to fight reality and win, but we can adapt if we are willing to give ourselves grace.

Showing ourselves compassion means we are willing to share our burdens and allow other people to help us carry them. Sometimes the things that are too heavy for us to carry on our own become manageable with the support of others.

No matter what phase of life we are in, having our needs met is a communal effort because there is only so much we can accomplish on our own. We need to be getting our needs met at least eighty percent of the time in order to have a wide enough window of tolerance. Our window of tolerance determines how greatly situations affect us. Knowing what our needs are isn't enough. We need to also know what the main obstacles are to our needs getting met. This helps us to be better prepared for moments of distress.

Just as there are four core human needs, there are also four main obstacles that can prevent us from getting our needs met. Two of them are completely out of our control. Two of them we have some control over. How we handle them either leaves us feeling more in our power or drains us. Let's explore each one.

Outside of Our Control Are People and Circumstances

People

Sometimes people are unable to care for us and/or they need us to take care of them. Sometimes there will be people we cannot rely on to get our needs met. We have varying degrees of dependency on others at different times in our lives. A small child, a disabled, or elderly person, is very dependent on others for their needs. Someone who is incapable of processing their emotions is also dependent on other people to get their needs met. They lack the internal resources to take good care of themselves.

This is something we need to accept as part of life. We have to be mindful that when we have unrealistic expectations of other people, we become resentful. For example, I don't expect my young child to provide my basic sustenance and security needs. I also don't expect someone who lacks emotional maturity to be a source of emotional support for me. But this wasn't always the case. For the longest time, I was ignorant of the fact that not everyone was equipped to support me. I didn't realize that I wasn't tied to one specific source of support and care. If my need wasn't getting met, I had options. I could collaborate or look to other healthier sources.

In relationships, each individual requires a network of healthy sources for their needs to ensure that they have the capacity to be there for another individual. One person cannot be the only source for another person's needs. It really does take a village. As adults with agency, we have the freedom to decide who we turn to for connection and support. If we fixate on one person to be the source of your needs, we give our power away. It is our responsibility to identify the people we can rely on (not how we want people to *change* to suit our needs). We prioritize the relationships that are best for our overall well-being.

Circumstances

The next main obstacle that can prevent us from having our needs met is circumstances or events. For example, if your home is destroyed in a natural disaster or forces in positions of authority have created an unsafe environment, these circumstances are outside of your control.

We can't control the family or political status we are born into, and we sometimes are faced with making a bad decision or a worse decision through no fault of our own. Our choices are only as good as our options. When I was in active addiction, my choices each day were: to be unable to function because of all the unprocessed trauma I was carrying, or use a substance that would make living feel somewhat bearable. Neither option was ideal, but at the time, I had no support to create another option.

We will always make the best choices we can with the skills, tools, and awareness we have. However, we don't all have the same options at the same time. This is where it becomes so important to be compassionate toward ourselves and focus on our core needs of safety, sustenance, and connection as much as we can. Having these needs met in some capacity will allow us to get through really difficult times.

Remember that our personal power – our energy – is limited, and the past and present already exist. Instead of using our energy to resist our present circumstances, we want to use our energy on the things within our control that can help us create a different future.

(Somewhat) Within Our Control Are Our Beliefs and Actions

Beliefs

It's no secret that how we feel about things impacts our judgment, our decisions, and our actions. **Our feelings are our beliefs.** They are what we think things mean and what we think is true. We are not in full control of these beliefs. They are inherited or established based on our past experiences.

The stronger the visceral response, the more powerful the belief, which is why simply changing our thoughts is not going to change how we feel. It may temporarily change the mood state we are in, but it does not rewire the belief, which is built into our nervous system.

Outrunning Your Emotions

Many people think we can change our beliefs simply by repeating a statement over and over. This may lead us to shifting our mentality over time, but the more powerful form of belief-shifting is through a process known as autosuggestion. This is a psychological technique developed by Dr. Emilie Coué[33]. It is the process of consciously or deliberately programming ourselves with new beliefs.

Most people think the technique works because we choose a new thought and repeatedly believe it, but really, it only works if we say *yes* to the new thought, and we are only able to agree to a new thought when our body is in a regulated state.

When Dr. Coué was using autosuggestions on his patients, he first had them enter a relaxed, trance-like state. He understood that they needed to feel safe physically in order to be open mentally. If we are in a subconsciously defensive or protective state, our mind will reject the new idea.

When our mind rejects a new thought (i.e., a different perspective), it is because we are attached to the agreements we've made with those thoughts. There is safety and familiarity with our old thoughts. Our beliefs give us certainty. It's not easy for us to just let go of old stories because our stories are the basis on which we approach our lives.

When we hold on to old ways of seeing the world, it can prevent us from getting the care we need or from taking care of ourselves. For example, if I was hurt by someone in the past and decide that it means that no one is trustworthy, I am going to be closed off from seeking or receiving support when I need it in future.

We are not victims of our beliefs. While we may not be in control of the unconscious and subconscious process that happens, we can use the Mighty Emotions Method ™ to process what we feel and get clarity on the way we have been interpreting the events in our lives. From this space of wisdom, we can see things differently and in ways that are more supportive of us having our needs met.

Actions

If we never adjust our actions to our present circumstances, our own behaviour can become an obstacle to having our needs satisfied. How we needed to behave in the past may no longer serve us in the present. Our actions can sometimes be deliberate, but more often than not, they are reactions to an experience we had, but never truly processed and resolved. We may have outgrown our default behaviour without even realizing. What is familiar to us will always be the path of least resistance.

Outrunning Your Emotions

This is the behaviour we will default to when we are stressed and unable to think clearly.

Living a fulfilling life is going to come with a certain level of risk. We must be willing to experiment with different actions if we want to experience different results. We can't get our present-day needs met if we continue to allow our past to dictate our present and determine our future. For example, if we withdraw from people because we are afraid of getting hurt again, we miss out on opportunities to get our need for connection met.

Are there certain behaviours you engage in that make you uncomfortable or unhappy? If guilt is showing up, it is signalling that you need to look at your behaviour. If you feel trapped and powerless, it's likely due to inaction. We don't realize how much emotional suffering is found in stagnation. Being at a plateau or feeling stuck in the same state for a long time means our need for meaning isn't being satisfied.

Our actions can produce results that impact our overall well-being and the well-being of others. They can be an indication of where we still have unprocessed experiences. While willpower and discipline have their purpose, sustainable change happens from the inside-out.

Why is it so hard to change?

When we don't practise processing our emotions, we live fearful lives. This is because we never learn to conquer our internal discomfort and regain our personal power. When we feel powerless, we avoid active change. Processing our emotions is key to navigating change from an empowered place.

Ignorance and defiance are enemies of improvement. When we are unaware or uninformed, we don't have what we need to make enlightened decisions. When we are unwilling to do things differently, even once shown a new way, our behaviour becomes self-destructive.

Fear is there to help us collaborate with change. It shows us what needs to be conquered, something we can only do by taking new and different actions and being open to the results. We work so hard to avoid pain that we miss out the gifts that life has for us. You can't have your cake and eat it too. We can't expect to heal and feel better, while simultaneously only taking the same actions or refusing to change our beliefs. We must be willing to accept the unknown if we don't want the future to feel like the past.

What about the "victim mentality"?

Someone is a victim the moment they experience harm, whether that harm is caused by other people, whether that's a result of our circumstances, whether it's due to our feelings or our actions. None of us can escape harm in life because not having our needs met is a form of harm.

When people refer to the "victim mentality", they are referring to someone believing they have no agency in life. They see themselves as powerless and view the actions of others as personal attacks toward them. This belief is one of the obstacles that can prevent them from having their needs met. They may also use this as an unhealthy way to try and get their needs met through the sympathy and kindness of others.

When we have been victimized, that is the time where we need to show ourselves compassion, not judge ourselves for having a "victim mentality". Your experience is real. Your pain is real, and it needs to be acknowledged so it can be processed, integrated, and resolved. We are victims, but we can become victorious.

Letting Ourselves Be Human

The purpose of understanding our emotions is to give ourselves permission to have the emotions that come with being impacted by life, and to understand how to take care of ourselves as human beings with needs. We do not need to be unaffected by the things that happen to us in life in order to be well.

People think stoicism is the pinnacle of emotional intelligence. This idea that we must endure hardship while pretending it doesn't affect us emotionally only further causes us harm. We are human. Life can be hard enough without us also being hard on ourselves.

Self-compassion is about having the power to punish ourselves and instead choosing to be sympathetic. It is about being understanding and tolerant toward ourselves. Tolerance is about the willingness to acknowledge what is, even if you disagree with it. Compassion is embracing the fact that everyone has unseen reasons for why they behave in a certain way. It's about being curious about what led someone to react a certain way rather than just penalizing behaviour. We have to allow ourselves and others to be flawed and give ourselves space to learn and improve.

We still need to hold ourselves and others accountable for our behaviour, but we can do so in a way that is more loving, open-minded and allows for deeper change. Modifying behaviour is not the same as actually reforming it. Reforming our behaviour is changing it from the core, addressing whatever underlying feeling or emotion was behind it in the first place. It is the difference between acting and amending.

Creating a Fulfilling Life

Designing your life in a way that allows your needs to be met is the key to living a good life. The exact mechanics of it look different for each of us, but at the core, it is always about safety, freedom, meaning, and connection.

We don't necessarily need to strive for balance (meaning that all areas of our lives are equal), but we do want to strive for harmony, meaning each area of our life is satisfied to an appropriate degree based on what we are most needing at the time, and none are neglected.

Creating a fulfilling life requires us to constantly look at what needs are more important to us and where we need to compromise. Discomfort is going to happen. It's part of outgrowing the different phases of our lives. We're not always paying attention to the natural progression of growth that we are experiencing. We should expect to outgrow who we are as individuals and how we see our world. Not allowing this growth to happen causes mental, emotional and spiritual suffering.

Even when a person, situation, feeling, or behaviour hinders us from getting our needs met, focusing on the need and not the obstacle is how we get back into alignment. We surrender, accept what has happened and adapt to a new reality. In recovery groups, we refer to this as *living life on life's terms*. Alignment isn't about only being at peace when life is meeting our expectations. It's about knowing how to find peace even amidst the chaos. In a fulfilling life, there will always be unfulfilling moments. By facing our feelings, finding our power, and loving ourselves, these moments don't have to overshadow our lives.

I often hear that there is "no end to healing". My experience has been different. Through practising the Mighty Emotions Method™ I have been able to change my relationship to the past, give myself what I need, and create a beautiful life. Since I started consistently checking in with my body, listening to my emotions, and taking aligned action, I've never had to return to the darkness that once consumed my days. I now know that waking up happy every day is a possible reality.

Outrunning Your Emotions

These tools have helped my clients find joy again as well. They've learned to be comfortable with their emotions and mature in ways avoiding their emotions had kept them from being. This has had a positive impact in all areas of their lives, but mostly importantly in their mental health.

I want this book to be a resource for you. When you are struggling with an emotion, or you want to help someone you love who is struggling, these are the basic principles that you can return to over and over, and they will assist you each time without fail:

- There is no such thing as an inappropriate or negative emotion. Every emotion is information of where we have an unmet need.
- We cannot reframe our thinking until we have regulated our body.
- Living beyond survival requires safety, freedom, meaning, and connection.
- When we focus on the things within our control and adapt to the things outside of our control, we regain our power.
- Each of us is inherently worthy and deserving of having our needs met. When we can be gentle with ourselves, we can create fulfilling lives.

What Now?

Now my friend, it's time to do the work. It's time to take action. Trust me when I say that knowledge without action is painful. It's not enough to know what our needs are, we have to actively pursue them in healthy, intentional ways. Now that we know our emotions are responses to our needs not being met and we have the steps to move through them (noticing, honouring, listening & responding), it's time to take action.

I'm not using this book to sell a course or a program or even my 1:1 coaching. I wrote this book because I wanted you to have this knowledge to put into practice. Unfortunately, it is useless just staying on these pages. Their real use is in the application of them to your life. To the challenging moments. To the everyday discomfort.

Being kinder to yourself when you are having a difficult time. Releasing the stories that are preventing you from having the love, connection and fulfilment you deserve.

Of course if you feel like you need accountability or more support, you can check out the resources section at the back. You can read any of the books I've referenced throughout these pages, and I suggest that you do because each of them helped me see life differently. What's most important is to remember that it is in *responding* to life differently that we heal and grow.

If I can go from being a homeless and hopeless drug addict to a well-adjusted wife, mother and human today, take that as proof that none of us are so broken that we cannot heal. If I can learn to embrace and love my discomfort even after spending a decade anaesthetizing myself with drugs and alcohol, take that as proof that there isn't a single emotion that will kill you if you face it, but not facing it might.

Life can get better for all of us both in what we experience and in how we feel about it. Please give yourself grace. Be gentle with yourself. Return to this book as many times as you need. Return to it when you need help understanding how to help someone who might be communicating through their behaviours or words that they have unmet needs. Listen to your emotions. Trust them! Because like Rumi famously wrote in the poem

Outrunning Your Emotions

The Guest House "The dark thought, the shame, the malice, meet them at the door laughing and invite them in. Be grateful for whoever comes because each has been sent as a guide from beyond."

Love your coach,
Jiselle

Acknowledgments

This book would not have been made possible without the support of the incredible people in my life. Firstly, to my husband Dylan, for not only always encouraging me, but for stepping up and taking over a great deal of the parenting while I would sneak off to get parts of this book done. I would not have even eaten at times if you did not bring food to my desk. I love you so much. You are the best partner and father I could have asked for.

To my daughter Kira for being the catalyst of change in my life. Giving birth to you awakened a purpose in me for the world, I want to leave behind for you. A world that is more empathic and kind. I hope you always know how much I have learned from watching you grow.

To my sponsor and life mentor, Ms. Rhonda, I am so grateful for the emotional support and encouragement you offer me. Thank you for always reminding me to bring God into the equation and not to settle for the bare minimum in life. You are my family & I am forever grateful that I am safe to be human with you.

To my friends, my ROD, Dani, Kabibi, Shar, Cat and all who have listened to me speak about my dreams for years and continued to cheer me on as I have worked on this book, thank you! You are some of the best human beings I have ever had the privilege to meet. Thank you for letting me be there for you as well. It is a blessing to have these healthy, reciprocal relationships in my life.

To my clients, thank you for the honour of being your coach. Being able to support you when you struggle, celebrate you when you thrive and through it all watch you grow means the world to me. You did the work and allowed me to hold up the mirror so you could see the beauty inside of you all along. Thank you for allowing me to share some of the work we've done together in this book.

Outrunning Your Emotions

To my editor, Clara Abigail for being the most kindred soul to review my work. Thank you for steering the ship and always reminding me to write for the reader. This work could not have been what it is without your collaboration.

To you, the reader, whether you purchased this book yourself or received it as a gift, THANK YOU for giving these words a home. I did not write this book for me. I wrote it for *you*. I hope that more than anything else, this book gives you permission to be a flawed, but beautiful human being. I hope you know that you are not broken. You can have a life that feels good and more than anything you are worthy of that.

Finally, to my former self, thank you for not giving up even when you didn't see a bright future, you believed better was possible and were willing to keep searching for it. Without the pain and lessons learned, this book wouldn't be possible. May it be my service to the world.

About the Author

As an emotions coach and advocate for mental & emotional well-being, Jiselle Gilliard Jegousse is on a mission to help individuals harness the power of their emotions and find inner peace. It was on her own journey of overcoming drug addiction, anxiety and depression, that she discovered the transformative power of making peace with one's emotions and tapping into their inherent wisdom.

Drawing from her background as a certified emotions coach and her extensive training in positive psychology, psychological first-aid and emotional CPR, Jiselle offers practical tools, compassionate guidance, and a safe space for individuals to explore their emotional landscapes. Jiselle's coaching approach is centred on empowering empathic souls to embrace their emotions as a source of strength and growth. She believes that our emotions are not something to be feared or suppressed but are powerful messengers guiding us toward our true selves.

Outrunning Your Emotions

In addition to her coaching practice, Jiselle is the host of *The Mighty Emotions Podcast,* spreading her message of hope and resilience to audiences worldwide. Her first book *Your Emotions Are Powerful and So Are You* is available for download free inside her online community; a safe space for anyone struggling to simply show up and be human.

Her second book *Outrunning Your Emotions* is a heartfelt and empowering guidebook for anyone who feels burdened by their emotional struggles and wants to live a more peaceful and fulfilling life.

If you're ready to embark on a transformative journey toward emotional freedom, Jiselle Gilliard Jegousse is the trusted guide that will walk alongside you every step of the way. With her compassionate support and unwavering belief in your potential, she will help you make peace with your emotions, uncover your inner power, and discover the boundless possibilities that await you on the path to self-discovery.

Connect with Jiselle
Website: Mightyemotions.com
IG & Tik Tok: @mighty_emotions
Email: mightyemotions@gmail.com

Appendix A: Ways of Honouring Your Emotions

We honour our emotions by allowing the energy in our bodies to flow. This means becoming present with the physical sensations in our bodies rather than contracting and trying to stimulate our minds. Here is a non-exhaustive list of ways we can honour our emotions:

To honour heavy emotions	To honour active emotional energy
<ul><li>Lightly tap the tips of your fingers up and down the length of your legs while in a seated position</li><li>Shake out your hands</li><li>Make tiny circles with your wrists in both directions</li><li>Rub your wrists one at a time</li><li>In a seated position, cross your arms across your chest with your hand to the opposite shoulder and cross your ankles</li></ul>	<ul><li>Wiggle your toes</li><li>Get up and dance</li><li>Go for a walk or run</li><li>Physical exercise</li><li>Tense all of your muscles, hold for a few seconds, then release</li><li>Humming: you can try humming for 4 counts followed by a deep inhale or you can listen to relaxing music and hum along to it/make up your own song to the instrumental</li></ul>

This list is merely a sample of the many ways we can connect with our bodies, allowing our energy to move and our emotions to flow. We may even notice that we have small habits that are actually our way of seeking to self-soothe/regulate when we are stressed.

Please note that emotional release may occur as a result of these actions. Release can look like crying, yawning, physically shaking, etc. This is the natural reaction of the body when we allow stagnant energy to flow.

For more tips on processing and honouring your emotions, head to mightyemotions.com

Appendix B: Core Needs Wheel

The Core Needs Wheel™ is a tool you can use to help you identify where your needs are not being met.

How to use:
- Starting with one area of the wheel at a time, rate how much your need is being met by colouring in the lines corresponding with the numbers 1-10 (One= this need is not being met at all, Ten =this need is being met completely)
- Once all sections have been coloured in, look at the areas with the lowest rating and complete the following sentences:
    - The need I most need to focus on is....
    - Some healthy ways I can get this need met is...
    - In the coming weeks, I will work on getting this need met by....

Complete the exercise as many times as you need to. As you begin to take action and get your needs met more, you will notice a significant difference in your dominant thoughts & emotions.

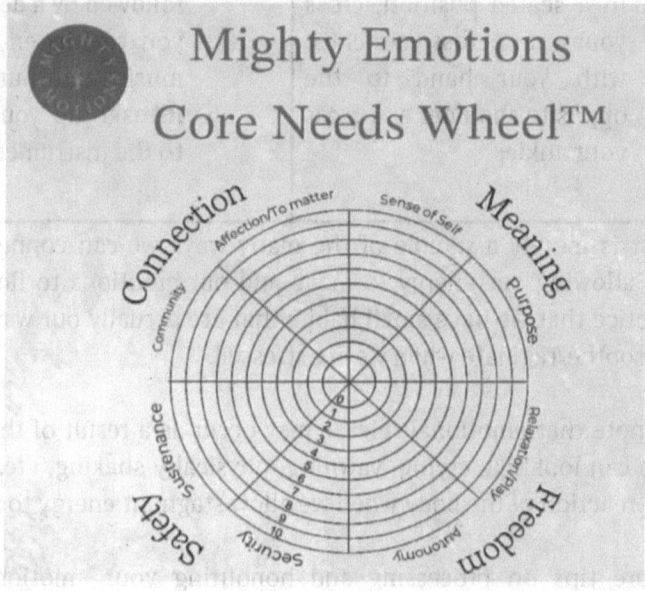

To Download the Core Need Wheel™, head to members.mightyemotions.com

Appendix C: Expanded Needs List

This table is meant to demonstrate how our core needs are met in various ways. It is not a complete list, and is meant to be used as a starting point when first understanding how to get our needs met.

Safety	Freedom	Meaning	Connection
Sustenance Needs *Food* *Clothing* *Water* *Shelter* *Vitamins* *Sleep* *Physical movement* Security *Physical safety* *Structure* *Order* *Consistency*	Independence *Autonomy* *Choice* *Space* *Agency* Fun *Pleasure* *Relaxation* *Laughter/Humor* *Restoration* *Freedom from responsibility*	Self-Esteem *Self-respect* *Self-Acceptance* *Self-Compassion* *Personal Growth* *Clear on values* Learning *Clarity* *Discovery* *Goals* *Challenge* Spirituality *Having a Higher Power* *Purpose* *Intention*	To Self & To Others *Support* *Empathy* *Kindness* *Intimacy* *Equality* *Presence* To Higher Power *Spiritual practice* *Guiding Principles* *Appreciation* *Humility* *Appreciation*

Appendix D: Sample Values List

Our values are the things that are important to us. When we need to make decisions, it is helpful to know what our values are so we can assess our options and make the choice that is most aligned. Here is a list of 100 qualities that might be important to you. These can change at different times in our lives and will often be prioritized by importance at any given moment. Look for the qualities you admire in others or you expect from others. These are examples of what you value.

1. Honesty
2. Loyalty
3. Abundance
4. Caring
5. Respect
6. Courage
7. Generosity
8. Gratitude
9. Openness
10. Accountability
11. Compassion
12. Success
13. Self-love
14. Spirituality
15. Forgiveness
16. Faith
17. Beauty
18. Humor
19. Prosperity
20. Change
21. Gracefulness
22. Peace
23. Harmony
24. Fun
25. Independence
26. Efficiency
27. Fairness
28. Accuracy
29. Humility
30. Decisiveness
31. Order
32. Clarity
33. Cleanliness
34. Optimism
35. Bravery
36. Friendliness
37. Selflessness
38. Trust
39. Thoughtfulness
40. Deep Connections
41. Patience
42. Reciprocity
43. Clear Communication
44. Passion
45. Patience
46. Confidence
47. Affection
48. Quality Time
49. Dedication
50. Reliability
51. Empathy
52. Stability
53. Tolerance
54. Emotional Intelligence
55. Gentleness
56. Warmth
57. Cooperation
58. Sweetness
59. Intimacy
60. Gift-Giving
61. Showing Appreciation
62. Mutual Support
63. Timeliness
64. Growth
65. Diversity
66. Teamwork
67. Work-Life Balance
68. Ingenuity
69. Professionalism
70. Recognition
71. Power
72. Work Ethic
73. Self-Development
74. Responsibility
75. Credibility
76. Encouragement
77. Adaptability
78. Service to Others
79. Dependability
80. Fast Pace
81. Positive Impact
82. Problem-Solving
83. Self-Discipline
84. Family
85. Friendship
86. Positivity
87. Freedom
88. Creativity
89. Happiness
90. Adventure
91. Balance
92. Wellness
93. Health and Fitness
94. Spontaneity
95. Travel
96. Financial Security
97. Self-Control
98. Conformity
99. Non-Conformity
100. Sustainability

Appendix E: Recognizing Our Emotions

This table is a cheat sheet to help you recognize your emotional experience and see what may need to be processed. Remember, while they are neatly separated in this table, in real life we often experience many emotions at once in addition to feelings that can leave us confused. Use this table to help you focus and identify which emotion(s) are impacting you. As needed return to the chapter on that emotion to walk you through the steps of honouring, listening & responding in an aligned way.

Sadness	We recognize sadness by the heaviness it carries. The weight of sadness is different depending on the intensity of it, but the essence of it is the same. Sadness causes us to slow down. Maybe we procrastinate or feel a lack of motivation. We may even feel stuck in some way or have no desire to move or take action. Sadness leaves clues in our behaviours. We find ourselves seeking comfort, whether it is through comfort eating or taking a nap or reaching for something to numb ourselves. We may listen to melancholy music or desire to sleep more or rest more. We can locate sadness by noticing how we feel in our center of the body. We may feel a tightness or heaviness in our chest or in our heart. Once we are aware that sadness is present, we can start to honour it.
Shame	Shame physically causes us to shrink ourselves. We may lower our eyes, cross our arms, or perform another self-pacifying behaviour. Physically, we feel shame in our gut. It's an uncomfortable "icky" feeling that we have trouble describing. When shame is present, typically we want to avoid interactions with other people. If we do need to be in social settings, we may feel the need to perform and put on a mask around others. We become hyper-focused on looking for cues that others approve of us.

Appendix E (Cont)

Guilt	Guilt feels like a combination of sadness and shame. There's a heaviness to it, but also a discomfort that makes us want to shrink ourselves. When guilt shows up, we may become really defensive in our interactions. We may also be avoidant and externally behave in a state of denial. Internally, we can find ourselves being really negative and critical of ourselves. We might beat ourselves up mentally, lecture and punish ourselves for not doing better. We might feel the weight of the world on our shoulders.
Fear	When we feel fear, there can be a surge of adrenaline and cortisol, causing us to panic or feel a sense of urgency. We may speed up and want to rush through our actions. Our heart starts beating faster. Our breathing becomes quicker and shorter, and we are unable to feel at ease in our bodies. Fear causes us to naturally have protective behaviours. We also know these are trauma responses. If we find ourselves behaving in one of the following ways, we are likely dealing with fear: Fight - we become defensive or aggressive, Flight - we want to hide and avoid a situation, Freeze - we feel paralyzed, confused, or indecisive, Fawn - we abandon ourselves and submit to the demands of others, Flock - we go along with the thinking of the group and match our behaviour to fit in with the crowds, and/or Focus - we become obsessive and hyper-focused on one element of our circumstances.
Anger	Anger literally creates heat in our bodies.[29] Our heart rate increases when we are angry and creates a rise in blood pressure and body temperature. We feel a surge of energy as hormones like adrenaline and cortisol are released, similar to fear. If we always suppress our anger, we can feel like our muscles are tense. We may cry as a way of our body releasing the emotions we are suppressing. Anger can be very subtle. We can be really closed off or rude to others, especially when we are trying to control and suppress our anger. It can also be intense and explosive, and we can feel out of control. We can yell or raise our voices. We may have an urge to cause someone harm or cause ourselves harm, and we might throw or slam or kick things in an attempt to get the anger out of our bodies.

Appendix E (Cont)

Disgust	Disgust can feel similar to fear or anger. Our heart rate can increase, we can contract our muscles and feel tenseness in our bodies. There can be a feeling of revulsion and wanting to crawl out of our skin. We may feel a strong need to control the situation at hand when we feel disgust. Our natural reaction to disgust is one of vengeance. We want to retaliate toward what appears unjust by our standards. We can be hyper judgemental or critical of others or ourselves. We can be really defiant and adamant that things be done our way. We become uncooperative when we experience disgust because of the lack of psychological safety we feel when our realities aren't aligned with our expectations.
Alignment	Alignment is defined as the state of being calm, peaceful and untroubled; a state of serenity. It's not achieved by accident. We have to put in effort (i.e., take aligned action) to create an aligned life. Most of us don't realise when we are in an aligned state because it feels mundane. We aren't accustomed to serenity.

Endnotes

1. Volkov, Sergey. "Mental health." *World Health Organization (WHO)*, 2023, https://www.who.int/health-topics/mental-health#tab=tab_2. Accessed 28 March 2023.
2. "Global prevalence and burden of depressive and anxiety disorders in 204 countries and territories in 2020 due to the COVID-19 pandemic." *The Lancet*, 29 July 2022, https://www.thelancet.com/journals/lancet/article/PIIS0140-6736(21)02143-7/fulltext. Accessed 22 April 2023.
3. Washington, Nicole. "Do Sociopaths Feel Empathy and Remorse?" *Psych Central*, 27 September 2022, https://psychcentral.com/health/psychopathy-and-feelings#do-sociopaths-have-feelings. Accessed 28 March 2023.
4. Brown, Brené. *Atlas of the Heart: Mapping Meaningful Connection and the Language of Human Experience*. Random House Publishing Group, 2021.
5. Lansley, Harry. "What are 7 Universal Facial Expressions?" *Emotional Intelligence Academy*, 16 April 2018, https://www.eiagroup.com/facial-expressions-explored/. Accessed 28 March 2023.
6. CDC, Healthly Development Basics. "Child Development Basics." *CDC*, 2023, https://www.cdc.gov/ncbddd/childdevelopment/facts.html. Accessed 28 March 2023.
7. Brown, Stuart. "Play deprivation has long term impacts on early child development." *Child & Family Blog*, 2018, https://childandfamilyblog.com/play-deprivation-early-child-development/. Accessed 28 March 2023.
8. Bhagat, Vidya, et al. "Emotional maturity of medical students impacting their adult learning skills in a newly established public medical school at the east coast of Malaysian Peninsula." *PubMed*, 14 October 2016, https://pubmed.ncbi.nlm.nih.gov/27790052/. Accessed 28 March 2023.
9. Teicher, Martin H et al. "Childhood maltreatment is associated with reduced volume in the hippocampal subfields CA3, dentate gyrus, and subiculum." Proceedings of the National Academy of Sciences of the United States of America vol. 109,9 (2012): E563-72. doi:10.1073/pnas.1115396109
10. Oldroyd, Kristina, et al. "A Model for Basic Emotions Using Observations of Behavior in Drosophila." *Frontiers*, 21 March 2019, https://www.frontiersin.org/articles/10.3389/fpsyg.2019.00781/full. Accessed 28 March 2023.
11. "The Difference Between Feelings and Emotions | WFU Online." *Wake Forest Online Counseling Program*, 2020, https://counseling.online.wfu.edu/blog/difference-feelings-emotions/. Accessed 28 March 2023.
12. Ackerman, Courtney E., and William Smith. "What are Positive and Negative Emotions and Do We Need Both?" *PositivePsychology.com*, 27 April 2019, https://positivepsychology.com/positive-negative-emotions/#differences. Accessed 28 March 2023.
13. Cherry, Kendra. "What Are Emotions? Types of Emotions in Psychology." *Verywell Mind*, 25 February 2022,

https://www.verywellmind.com/what-are-emotions-2795178. Accessed 29 March 2023.

14. Boag, Simon. "Conscious, preconscious, and unconscious — Macquarie University." *Macquarie University*, 2020, https://researchers.mq.edu.au/en/publications/conscious-preconscious-and-unconscious. Accessed 29 March 2023.

15. Rice, Nancy E. "Semiotics | Definition, Theory, Examples, & Facts | Britannica." *Encyclopedia Britannica*, 24 February 2023, https://www.britannica.com/science/semiotics. Accessed 29 March 2023.

16. Spinoza, Baruch. "Quote by Baruch Spinoza: "Emotion, which is suffering, ceases to be suffe..."" *Goodreads*, N/A, https://www.goodreads.com/quotes/1260693-emotion-which-is-suffering-ceases-to-be-suffering-as-soon. Accessed 29 March 2023.

17. Medline Plus, Stress and your health. "Stress and your health." *MedlinePlus*, 30 April 2022, https://medlineplus.gov/ency/article/003211.htm. Accessed 29 March 2023.

18. Fogel, Alan, and Alan Fogel's. "Emotional and Physical Pain Activate Similar Brain Regions." *Psychology Today*, 19 April 2012, https://www.psychologytoday.com/ca/blog/body-sense/201204/emotional-and-physical-pain-activate-similar-brain-regions. Accessed 29 March 2023.

19. Jacobs Hendel, Hilary. *It's Not Always Depression: Working the Change Triangle to Listen to the Body, Discover Core Emotions, and Connect to Your Authentic Self*. Random House Publishing Group, 2018. "The Change Triangle(R)" is a registered trademark of Hilary Jacobs Hendel and "It's Not Always Depression" (C) is a copyright of Change Triangle LLC 2018

20. Good Therapy, Window of Tolerance. "Window of Tolerance." *GoodTherapy*, 8 August 2016, https://www.goodtherapy.org/blog/psychpedia/window-of-tolerance. Accessed 29 March 2023.

21. APA Dictionary of Psychology. Mood. American Psychological Association.

22. Frankl, Viktor E. *Man's Search for Meaning*. Translated by Ilse Lasch, et al., Beacon Press, 2006.

23. Souders, Beata, and Maike Neuhaus. "What is Motivation? A Psychologist Explains." *PositivePsychology.com*, 5 November 2019, https://positivepsychology.com/what-is-motivation/#definition. Accessed 30 March 2023.

24. Aron, Elaine. *The Highly Sensitive Person: How to Thrive When the World Overwhelms You*. Harmony/Rodale, 1997.

25. Complex-post-traumatic stress disorder, Mind. "What is complex PTSD?" *Mind*, 2021, https://www.mind.org.uk/information-support/types-of-mental-health-problems/post-traumatic-stress-disorder-ptsd-and-complex-ptsd/complex-ptsd/. Accessed 30 March 2023.

26. Good Therapy, Window of Tolerance. "Window of Tolerance." *GoodTherapy*, 8 August 2016, https://www.goodtherapy.org/blog/psychpedia/window-of-tolerance. Accessed 29 March 2023.

27. adapted from The Personal Power Grid, in Managing Personal Change, by Cynthia Scott and Dennis Jaffe

28. Ahmad AH, Zakaria R. Pain in times of stress. *Malays J Med Sci*. 2015;22(Spec Issue):52–61.

29. Victoria State Government. "Anger - how it affects people." *Better Health Channel*, 30 03 2019, https://www.betterhealth.vic.gov.au/health/healthyliving/anger-how-it-affects-people. Accessed 26 April 2023.
30. Kahn, Matt. *Everything Is Here to Help You: A Loving Guide to Your Soul's Evolution.* Hay House, 2018. Accessed 1 July 2023.
31. Mills, Janet, and Don Miguel Ruiz. *The Four Agreements: A Practical Guide to Personal Freedom, Paperback.* Amber-Allen Publishing, 1997. Accessed 1 July 2023.
32. Rosenberg, Marshall B. *Nonviolent Communication: A Language of Life: Life-Changing Tools for Healthy Relationships.* PuddleDancer Press, 2015. *Amazon*, https://www.amazon.ca/Nonviolent-Communication-Language-Life-Changing-Relationships/dp/189200528X/ref=sr_1_1?crid=WX3XAQHXYTA2&keywords=Nonviolent+Communication%3A+A+Language+of+Life%3A&qid=1688216817&s=books&sprefix=nonviolent+communication+a+language+of+.
33. Coue, Emile. *Self Mastery Through Conscious Autosuggestion.* Digireads.com Publishing, 2006. Accessed 1 July 2023.

Also by Jiselle Gilliard Jegousse

Your Emotions are Powerful, but So Are You is 31 days of reflections and journal prompts to help you deepen your relationship with your emotions. Use this book as part of your daily self-check-in and watch how good your life begins to feel! Download the ebook at mightyemotions.com

Hear what readers had to say:

"This workbook will transform the way you relate to your emotions. It's practical, clear and engaging."

"Jiselle's workbook is what we all need when it comes to embracing all parts of ourselves and gaining deeper self-awareness. The compassionate and understanding tone will leave you feeling seen and heart."

For more free resources head to members.mightyemotions.com

www.ingramcontent.com/pod-product-compliance
Lightning Source LLC
Chambersburg PA
CBHW011315080526
44587CB00024B/4005